# THE HISTORIOGRAPHY
# OF THE AMERICAN
# CATHOLIC CHURCH: 1785-1943

# THE AMERICAN
# CATHOLIC TRADITION

*See last pages of this volume*
*for a complete list of titles.*

# THE HISTORIOGRAPHY
# OF THE AMERICAN
# CATHOLIC CHURCH: 1785-1943

JOHN PAUL CADDEN

## ARNO PRESS
A New York Times Company
New York ● 1978

Editorial Supervision: JOSEPH CELLINI

———◆———

Reprint Edition 1978 by Arno Press Inc.

Reprinted from a copy in the
    University of Illinois Library

THE AMERICAN CATHOLIC TRADITION
ISBN for complete set: 0-405-10810-9
See last pages of this volume for titles.

Manufactured in the United States of America

———◆———

**Library of Congress Cataloging in Publication Data**

Cadden, John Paul, 1913–
    The historiography of the American Catholic Church,
1785–1943.

    (The American Catholic tradition)
    Originally presented as the author's thesis, Catholic
University of America, 1943.
    Reprint of the 1944 ed. published by Catholic
University of America Press, Washington, which was
issued as no. 82 of Studies in sacred theology.
    Includes bibliographical references.
    1.  Catholic Church in the United States—Historio-
graphy.  2.  Catholic Church in the United States—
bibliography.  I, Title.  II.  Series,  III.  Series:
Catholic University of America.  School of Sacred
Theology.  Studies in sacred theology ; no. 82.
BX1406.C23  1978          016.282'73          77-11276
ISBN 0-405-10812-5

# THE HISTORIOGRAPHY
## OF THE
## AMERICAN CATHOLIC CHURCH: 1785–1943

This dissertation was conducted under the direction of the Right Reverend Monsignor Peter Guilday, J.U.D., F.H.R.S., as major Professor, and was approved by the Reverend William J. Lallou, S.T.D., and Professor Richard J. Purcell, Ph. D., LL.B., as Readers.

The Catholic University of America
Studies in Sacred Theology
Number 82

# THE HISTORIOGRAPHY OF THE AMERICAN CATHOLIC CHURCH: 1785-1943

BY

The Reverend John Paul Cadden, O.S.B., M.A., S.T.L.
St. Anselm's Priory
Brookland, D. C.

A DISSERTATION

Submitted to the Faculty of the School of Theology of the Catholic University of America in Partial Fulfillment of the Requirements for the Degree of Doctor of Sacred Theology

THE CATHOLIC UNIVERSITY OF AMERICA PRESS
WASHINGTON, D. C.
1944

*Imprimi Potest:*
  THOMAS V. MOORE, O.S.B.
    *Prior*
    St. Anselm's Priory

*Nihil Obstat:*
  PETER GUILDAY
    *Censor Deputatus*

*Imprimatur:*
  ✠ MICHAEL J. CURLEY
    *Archbishop of Baltimore-Washington*

December 1, 1943.

MURRAY & HEISTER—WASHINGTON, D. C.
PRINTED IN THE UNITED STATES OF AMERICA

# PREFACE

Students of American Catholic history have experienced a considerable waste of time and energy in their historical investigations because the literature has so long remained unanalyzed and uncatalogued.

Almost a quarter of a century ago Monsignor Peter Guilday recognized the need for a guide or bibliography which would aid students of the history of the Catholic Church in the United States in a way similar to the assistance rendered to the scholars of American history thirty years ago by the Channing-Hart-Turner *Guide to the Study and Reading of American History* (Boston, 1912). While carrying out his various historical projects, he prepared the foundation for such a guide by keeping on standard library cards all items of a purely bibliographical nature. With this nucleus, a systematic effort was made to extend the list to no less than a complete bibliography of American Catholic historical literature.

As a groundwork for the future guide, Dr. Guilday made from time to time surveys of an historiographical character. These include: "John Gilmary Shea," *Historical Records and Studies,* XVII (1926), 1–171, the only thorough biographical study that has been made of the Father of American Catholic history; "Lambing, Historian of Pittsburgh," *America,* L (December 16, 1933), 251–252; "Catholic Lay Writers of American Catholic History," *Catholic Historical Review,* XXIII (April, 1937), 52–62; "Catholic Historical Societies," *Official Catholic Year Book for 1928* (New York, 1928), 639–644; and three studies in the *Ecclesiastical Review:* (a) "Historians of the American Hierarchy," XCII (1925), 113–122; (b) "Recent Studies in American Catholic History," LXXXIV (1931), 528–546; (c) "The Writing of Parish Histories," XCIII (1935), 236–257. He also directed Father Adrian T. English's masters dissertation, presented in 1925 at The Catholic University of America and entitled: "The Historiography of American Catholic History (1785–1884)," and printed in the *Catholic Historical Review,* XI (January, 1926), 561–598.

Realizing that much of his time was being consumed in the preparation of his biography of Archbishop Hughes, Dr. Guilday turned over his entire bibliographical collection to the present writer in 1939 for the purpose of completing the long-desired guide.

During the past four years, an effort was made to expand the bibliography in a systematic fashion. The following procedure was adopted to insure, as far as possible, accuracy and completeness: material pertaining to the history of the Church in America in all American Catholic historical periodicals as well as in other important American historical journals was indexed on standard library cards. Similarly, material appearing in the leading American Catholic reviews other than historical, such as the *American Catholic Quarterly Review,* the *Catholic World,* the *Ecclesiastical Review, Thought,* and the *Central Blatt and Social Justice* was indexed. From the *Shelf List* of the Library of Congress, a catalogue of all books on the subject of American Catholic Church history was drawn up and, whenever possible, Library of Congress cards were purchased. Using this as a nucleus, the Guilday collection was incorporated, forming an extensive bibliography. A personal survey was then made of all doctoral and masters dissertations done in the leading Catholic colleges and universities of the country, and these were also incorporated.

With the index fairly complete, a plan was formed for the preparation of a practical guide to the literature. The completed volume will be divided into three parts: Part I is entitled: "American Catholic Historiography: 1785–1943," and is devoted to a description of the development that has taken place in American Catholic historical writing, with particular attention directed to the outstanding critical historians of the period. Part II will be entitled: "The Literature of American Catholic Church History," and will be a description and evaluation of the literature in the field, including all the important bibliographical aids. Part III will be a selected catalogue of approximately five thousand items on American Catholic Church History. A more detailed outline of the prospective volume follows:

## Part I

AMERICAN CATHOLIC HISTORIOGRAPHY: 1785–1943

A.  American Catholic Historiography: 1785–1884.
B.  John Gilmary Shea.
C.  Catholic Historical Societies.
D.  American Catholic Historiography: 1884–1915.
E.  American Catholic Historiography: 1915–1943.

## Part II

THE LITERATURE OF AMERICAN CATHOLIC
CHURCH HISTORY

A.  The General Guides to the Literature of American Catholic History.
B.  Expansion of the Church in America.
  1.  Missionary Literature.
      a.  Bibliographical aids.
      b.  Franciscan.
      c.  Jesuit.
      d.  Benedictine.
      e.  Dominican.
      f.  Other Missionary Orders.
  2.  Religious Orders of Women.
      a.  Bibliographical aids.
      b.  Ursuline Sisters.
      c.  Mercy Sisters.
      d.  Benedictine Sisters.
      e.  Dominican Sisters.
      f.  Sisters of Charity, etc.
C.  Church Foundations.
  1.  Provincial.
  2.  Archdiocesan.
  3.  Diocesan.
  4.  Parochial.
D.  Internal Organization.
  1.  Councils.
  2.  Problems: Trusteeism, Schisms, etc.
  3.  Anti-Catholic Literature.

E. Institutional and Cultural Development.
  1. Educational Institutions.
    a. Seminaries.
    b. Colleges and Universities.
    c. Secondary and Elementary Schools.
  2. Charitable Institutions.
  3. Art and Architecture.
F. Biography.
  1. Bibliographical Aids.
  2. Hierarchy.
    a. Cardinals.
    b. Apostolic Delegates.
    c. Archbishops.
    d. Bishops.
  3. Clergy (Diocesan).
  4. Clergy (Religious).
  5. Sisters.
  6. Laymen.
  7. Converts.

*Part III*

SELECTED CATALOGUE OF THE LITERATURE OF AMERICAN
CATHOLIC HISTORY

This monograph is Part One of the three parts as outlined above. Its purpose is to describe the development that has taken place in American Catholic historical writing by examining the outstanding critical Catholic historians of the period as well as the growth of certain Catholic historical institutions, such as the Catholic historical societies and the various seminars in history established at the leading Catholic universities and colleges. With the exceptions of The Catholic University of America, the University of Notre Dame, St. Louis University and Creighton University, surprisingly little research has been accomplished by historical seminars in the restricted field of American Church history.

Since this first part is confined to a description of the development that has taken place in American Catholic historical writing, the works of many outstanding non-Catholic historians touching on American Catholic Church history, such as Sweet, Gabriel, Greene, Will, Billington and others, will receive adequate notice in Part Two. The writings of many important contemporary Catholic historians will be reserved for a more detailed treatment in the second part.

To avoid the appearance of incompleteness which the separate publication of Part One will probably give to this work, it is noted here that an important section of Part Two is a lengthy treatment of all the important guides, both general and special, to American Catholic historical literature. This section includes a consideration of the archival centers both here and abroad. No bibliography has been appended to this dissertation; but a complete list of the literature cited will be given when the other parts of the work are completed.

The writer wishes to express his appreciation to his Superior, the Very Reverend Dom Thomas Verner Moore, O.S.B., Ph.D., M.D., who generously made this course of study possible. My interest in American Catholic historiography was first aroused by the lectures of Monsignor Peter Guilday, my major professor. The completion of the present undertaking is largely due to the encouragement, the skill, patience and goodwill of this master of American Church history who for several years has continuously guided my steps and enlarged my collectanea. I wish to pay especial homage to a number of other friends who, in their kindness, have found time to read the manuscript and to give me their comments. The writer is fully aware of the use which he has been able to make of their observations in diminishing many weaknesses in the original draft. Never to be forgotten are the detailed instructions and observations given to a youthful investigator by Professor Richard J. Purcell, Ph.D., LL.B. The Reverend William J. Lallou, S.T.D., formerly President of the American Catholic Historical Society of Philadelphia, and the Reverend John Tracy Ellis, Ph.D., have generously criticized the manuscript. At various time I have been aided also by Mr. Victor Shaefer, Head of the Preparations Department of the John K. Mullen Memorial Library at The Catholic University of America, who has shared with me his private collectanea and his special knowledge of the subject. For courteous aid in a variety of matters I am indebted also to the Reverend John E. Sexton, the Reverend Robert H. Lord, Ph.D., the late Reverend Raymond Corrigan, S.J., the Reverend William J. Kane, S.J., the Reverend Thomas A. McAvoy, C.S.C., the Reverend Victor F. O'Daniel, O.P., and to the Reverend Raphael Huber, O.F.M.

The writer also takes this opportunity of expressing his gratitude to the librarians and members of the staff of the libraries of the various institutions visited: The Library of Congress; Harvard University; St. John's Seminary, Brighton, Massachusetts; Detroit University; De Paul University; Loyola University; Notre Dame University; Creighton University; St. Louis University; Fordham University; Columbia University; Georgetown University; and the New York Public Library. At home, the staff of the John K. Mullen Memorial Library at The Catholic University of America has served me with flawless courtesy and skill.

To numerous friends in Boston, Detroit, Chicago, South Bend, Omaha, St. Louis, and New York I wish to express my gratitude for the charming courtesies and kind hospitality received during my sojourn as their guest.

In offering my thanks to those who have helped me, however, I must make clear that this does not involve them in any sort of responsibility for the following pages. For any defects, I alone am responsible.

REV. JOHN PAUL CADDEN, O.S.B.

*January 17, 1944.*

# TABLE OF CONTENTS

# CHAPTER I

## HISTORIOGRAPHY OF THE AMERICAN CATHOLIC CHURCH: 1785–1884

THE expansion of the Catholic Church during the first century of its existence in this country had a profound influence upon the advancement of American Catholic historical scholarship. The one hundred years that passed between the establishment of an organized hierarchy under Father John Carroll as prefect apostolic and the Third Plenary Council of Baltimore were years of intense activity within the Catholic Church itself. The first seven decades of the period, when the Church was striving to take root, were marked by continuous stress and insecurity occasioned by the social and political ostracism its members experienced at the hands of non-Catholics.[1] It was during these first seventy years that the outstanding figures in the Church devoted the greater part of their energies to the defense of the Catholic faith. It was during this time also that the Church underwent those acute internal disorders caused by the dearth of priests, trusteeism and mixed marriages. This same short span witnessed the public debates between Hughes and Breckenridge and Purcell and Campbell over the alleged incompatibility of Catholic principles with American democratic ideals.

At the same time, however, the organization of the Church, which had been loose in the first two decades, was attaining a unity and cohesion that was steadily becoming more and more defined. Much time and energy were expended on the uniformity of Church discipline; so much so, that during the years when the entire country was within the single province of Baltimore (1808–1846), no less than six provincial councils were held for

---

[1] Robert Gorman, *Catholic Apologetical Literature in the United States: 1784–1858* (Washington, D. C., 1939), 1–6.

1

this very purpose.[2]  Much attention was also focused on Catholic education and from the moment of the first legislative act of the Synod held ,in 1791, the Church made a concentrated effort to build up a school system exclusively Catholic.[3]

The last thirty years of the century (1785–1884) witnessed a transition that was marked by the Know-nothing campaign of the fifties and the rivalries and antagonisms of other anti-Catholic organizations.  Nevertheless, these were also years of a remarkable increase both in numbers and power.  The peaks of the growth in Catholic population came with successive waves of European immigrants.  In the decade 1840–1850 there was an increase of one million.  From 1850–1860 the increase was approximately two millions; and between 1870–1880 it had reached the remarkable figure of three millions.[4]  Simultaneously with this rapid rise in the population graph, there was on the part of the Church a constant acquisition and consolidation of property. Hand-in-hand with this went the construction of churches, rectories, schools, orphanages and hospitals which has given to this period the unlovely title of " brick-and-mortar " age.  Along with these great changes there was a gradual emergence of power that was making itself felt in the cultural and spiritual life of the nation.  This century of stress and change exercised an unwholesome influence in that it retarded intellectual development within the Catholic body.  There was little notable literary activity, particuarly in the field of historical studies.  Catholics found their activities cramped and their efforts to advance cruelly thwarted.  As a consequence they found little incentive to literary studies and few found the time to devote to historical re-

[2] Peter Guilday, *A History of the Councils of Baltimore: 1791–1884* (New York, 1932), 81–153. These provincial councils were held in 1829, 1833, 1837, 1840, 1843 and 1846.  When the seventh provincial council of Baltimore was held in 1849 the American Church consisted of three provinces: Baltimore, St. Louis and Oregon City.

[3] James A. Burns, *Growth and Development of the Catholic School System in United States* (New York, 1912).

[4] Gerald Shaughnessy, *Has the Immigrant Kept the Faith?* (New York, 1925), 189.

search.[5]  Under these conditions, it is not surprising to find rather desultory efforts made to record the history of the period and many of these early historical works were uncritical and unscientific and were intended primarily for edification.  The more creditable performances in the field of historical studies took the form of general surveys of the Church in the United States. These at their very best, with some exceptions in the form of historical documents, were below even the second-rate efforts of writers in the field of American history.  The exceptions alluded to are semi-narrative sources or Reports sent by members of the Catholic hierarchy to the Sacred Congregation de Propaganda Fide in Rome.

The earliest of these Reports is that of Father John Carroll written in answer to several official letters from Propaganda[6] requesting definite information regarding the state of the Church in the new Republic.  In an effort to give as complete a picture as possible, Carroll corresponded with his fellow-priests between November, 1784 and March 1, 1785.  The information he obtained was later embodied in his Report, which he entitled *Relatio Pro Emo. Cardinali Antonello de statu Religionis in Unitis Foederatae Americae provinciis.*[7]

This first Report to be sent to Rome from the United States is a treasured first-hand source for the history of the Church in our country.  It is divided into three sections.  The first section gives an account of the Catholic population in the United States; the second describes the conditions, piety, defects and other aspects of American Catholic life; the third section treats of the

---

[5] Adrian T. English, "Historiography of American Catholic History: 1785–1884," *Catholic Historical Review*, XI (January, 1926), 564–565.

[6] This information was asked through the Nuncio at Paris, on May 12, 1784, in a letter addressed by Cardinal Antonelli to the Chevalier de la Luzerne, French Minister Plenipotentiary at New York, and again in another letter from Cardinal Antonelli to Father Carroll dated June 9, 1784.

[7] The original Report is preserved in the archives of Propaganda and has been published by Peter Guilday in his *Life and Times of John Carroll* (New York, 1922), 223–227, together with a translation made by John Gilmary Shea.  The rough draft made by Carroll is in the Baltimore Cathedral archives, Case 9A–F1.

number of priests, their character and qualifications and their means of support. The Report is concise and to the point, and neither conceals nor exaggerates the desperate condition of the struggling Church in America.

The second of these important episcopal Reports is that of Benedict Joseph Flaget, Bishop of Bardstown.[8] Shortly after his consecration by Archbishop Carroll in 1810, Bishop Flaget spent a year in making a visitation of his vast diocese. The observations he made on this occasion are embodied in a remarkable source for this early period. It is addressed to Pope Pius VII under date of April 10, 1815. Bishop Flaget begins the letter with felicitations to His Holiness on the latter's release from captivity. He then describes the state of the Church in Kentucky, the number of priests and churches, the establishment of a seminary at Bardstown and the communities of religious women then settled in his diocese—the Sisters of Charity at Nazareth and the Sisters of Loretto at the Foot of the Cross of Jesus at Loretto. The Report concludes with a brief but adequate survey of the condition of the Church in other sections of his extensive diocese which included the states of Tennessee, Indiana, Illinois, Ohio and the great Northwest Territory.[9]

---

[8] Benedict Joseph Flaget came to the United States in 1792 as a member of the Society of Saint Sulpice. He was assigned to the mission of Vincennes until 1795 when he was called to Baltimore by Bishop Carroll and appointed to the faculty of Georgetown College. He held this post for three years and was then sent to Havana, Cuba, to assist in the establishment of a Sulpician college in that city. Returning to Baltimore in 1801, he taught in the seminary there for seven years. In 1808 he was transferred to Mount Saint Mary's College, Emmitsburg, Maryland, where he was stationed when he learned of his elevation to the newly erected see of Bardstown.

[9] Flaget's Report is in the archives of Propaganda (*Scritture riferite, America Centrale*, VII, fol. 323–326). For over thirty years the Report was either unknown or not available to historians; Bishop Martin J. Spalding, who availed himself of many other letters and documents, did not use it in his *Sketches of the Life, Times and Character of the Right Reverend Benedict Joseph Flaget, First Bishop of Bardstown* (Louisville, 1852). It is not mentioned in Benjamin Webb's *Centenary of Catholicity in Kentucky* (Louisville, 1884). It was first printed with translation and

The third Report, that of Archbishop Ambrose Maréchal of Baltimore,[10] was based upon the results of a questionnaire sent to his clergy and his own observations made on a personal visitation of his diocese.[11]  This information Archbishop Maréchal analyzed and summed up in his *Ratio status religionis Catholicae in diocesi Baltimorensi reddita ab Ambrosio Archiepiscopo 1818. Illustrissimo ac Eminentissimo Cardinali Litta. Praefecto Sacrae Congregationis Propagandae Fidei.*[12]  This Report is much longer than the other two, covering eighteen folio pages and is of paramount importance to the history of the Catholic Church in the United States. It is divided into nine sections, treating every phase of the American Church at that time: the number of priests, faithful and churches; seminaries and convents; the trying situations which the priests had to face and the character of some malcontents among them; the vices of the American people and the attitude of the Protestants towards the Church; the freedom of action given to the Church by American law; the internal difficulties arising within the Church, particularly the schisms in Norfolk and Charleston; the erection of new sees in Georgia and Louisiana; and the important difficulties which the growing Church had to face, especially from the dearth of priests

---

notes by Victor F. O'Daniel, O.P., *Catholic Historical Review*, I (October, 1915), 305–319.

[10] Archbishop Maréchal was a Sulpician. He came to the United States in 1792 and was engaged in pastoral work in the archdiocese of Baltimore until 1799. From 1799 to 1803, he was a member of the faculty of St. Mary's Seminary, Baltimore, Maryland, and of Georgetown College. For the next nine years he taught in several Sulpician seminaries in France. Upon his return to Baltimore in 1812, he was assigned to the faculty of St. Mary's Seminary, Baltimore, which post he held until 1817 when he was appointed coadjutor archbishop of Baltimore.

[11] The questionnaire is given in Peter Guilday, *The Church in Virginia: 1815–1822* (New York, 1924), 87.

[12] The original is in the archives of Propaganda. (*Scritture riferite, America Centrale,* IV, fol, 922) and is printed in full for the first time in the *Catholic Historical Review,* I (January, 1916), 439–453. Cf. Thomas Hughes, *History of the Society of Jesus in North America, Colonial and Federal* (New York, 1907–17), *Documents* I, part I, 245–246, 560; part II, 911–914, 957–958, 1049. A copy of the Report is among the Shea Transcripts in the Riggs Memorial Library at Georgetown University.

and the evils of lay trusteeism. Maréchal appended to his Report a catalogue of the priests in the archdiocese of Baltimore, which contains the names of eighteen Jesuits, nine Sulpicians and twenty-five diocesan priests.

Two pamphlets which appeared after Carroll's Report should be mentioned here, not for their inherent historical value, for they have none, but because they shed light upon the difficulties Carroll had to meet at the outset of his prefecture. Both pamphlets are an attack upon the suppressed Society of Jesus in the United States. The first, by the Reverend Patrick Smyth, is entitled *The Present State of the Catholic Mission Conducted by the Ex-Jesuits in North America* (Dublin, 1788). Smyth was an Irish secular priest who came to Baltimore in 1787 and was for some time a guest of Father John Carroll. The following year he returned to Ireland and published this attack upon his former host. The pamphlet is hardly more than a résumé of the charges that had been often lodged against the Jesuits. He accused the ex-Jesuits in Maryland of securing large landed estates and possessing Negro slaves, while they, the masters, passed their time attending to the religious needs of those dwelling in nearby towns or cities, doing nothing for the scattered Catholics settled beyond the borders of Maryland " refinement." [13] The final twenty pages of the forty-eight page pamphlet are devoted to an abusive attack on Father Carroll and William O'Brien, O.P., pastor of St. Peter's Church, New York City. Smyth presents several letters to support his charges, but all of them have been shown to be badly garbled versions.[14] The influence this diatribe had in Ireland and Rome was considerable. In Ireland it injured the good name of the American Church, while in Rome it created suspicions against the missionaries by false assertions; for example, that they had established a Jesuit novitiate, an act that would have been contrary to the bull of suppression which was in full effect at the time.

The work of Claude Florent Bouchard de la Poterie was also in the form of a pamphlet and entitled *The Resurrection of*

---

[13] English, *loc. cit.,* 570.
[14] *Ibid.,* 571–572.

*Laurent Ricci; or a True and Exact History of the Jesuits*
(Philadelphia, 1789). Poterie had served as chaplain in the
French forces under Rochambeau. Late in the year 1788 he
began to serve the mission in Boston, but his conduct forced
Father Carroll to suspend him in May of the following year.
He removed from Boston to Quebec but returned for a short
time before finally leaving the country in January, 1790. Before
his departure he published his attack on Father Carroll and the
priests of the American Church. The viciousness of the small
pamphlet of twenty-eight pages is clearly indicated in its dedication: " To the New Laurent Ricci in America, the Rev. Father
John Carroll, Superior of the Jesuits in the United States, also to
the friarinquisitor, William O'Brien." [15]   Father O'Brien had
been brought into the affair in 1789 when he was commissioned
to investigate Poterie's conduct. It was his report of the conditions which existed in Boston that led to the suspension of the
erratic priest.[16]   Poterie's pamphlet, like Smyth's work, is but a
summary of the scurrilous charges so often made against the
Jesuits. Four sentences only—two of them in a note—refer to
Jesuit activity in this country. It is a false history of their work
in other places and cannot in any sense be considered a history of
the Church or of the Jesuits in America.

The first serious attempt to compose a general history of the
Church in America was made by John Dilhet, S.S. Father Dilhet
was born at Toulouse, France, November 18, 1753. Soon after
his ordination in 1778 he entered the Sulpician solitude at Issy.
Between the years 1798 and 1807 he was a missionary in this
country. From 1798 to 1805 he was stationed at Detroit, and
then at Baltimore and in Pennsylvania. While on the mission in
Conewago, Pennsylvania, he co-operated with his confrere, Francis Charles Nagot, in the establishment of the college at Pigeon
Hills, Pennsylvania, which later was transferred to Emmitsburg,
Maryland, becoming the present Mount Saint Mary's College.[17]

---

[15] Father Lorenzo Ricci was the last Superior General (1758–1775) of
the Society of Jesus before the Suppression.

[16] Cf., Guilday, *Carroll,* 283–289.

[17] English, *loc. cit.,* 573–574. Cf.

Dilhet's general account of Catholicism in the United States is entitled: *État de l'Église Catholique, ou Diocèse des États-Unis de l'Amérique Septentrionale.* It is a manuscript volume in duodecimo, of 193 closely written pages, preserved in the archives of St. Mary's Seminary at Baltimore.[18]   It is not the original autograph but a copy, much of which is carelessly done.

Dilhet's purpose was to give a sketch of ecclesiastical developments during his nine years' residence in the United States, together with a résumé of the activities of the Catholic Church prior to the establishment of the American hierarchy.   His manuscript has three major divisions: (1) " Early Days of the Catholic Church in America; " (2) " The Establishment of the See of Baltimore; " (3) " The Catholic Missions and Congregations in the United States."   After some general remarks, Father Dilhet describes the whole area of the United States state by state, county by county in some instances, and mission by mission.   The earlier copyist, through error, interjected amid the counties of Maryland a valuable list of Catholic priests in the United States and the account of the mission at New Castle, Maine.   Dilhet's style, like that of so many writers of his period, is prolix and facts are frequently obscured by verbiage.   The work as a whole lacks continuity and repetitions are of frequent occurrence.   His judgment of men and events is frequently exaggerated and not in accord with present day demands of the canons of historical criticism.   His racial prejudices, particularly against German and Irish priests, enter into his field of vision.   He had not seen all the places of which he writes, and his observations are not always accurate, but, taken together, they cast a flood of light on the situation of the American Church at the beginning of the nineteenth century.   John Gilmary Shea used the manuscript, and regarded it as a document of prime importance.[19]

The next work of importance concerning the historical develop-

---

[18] A partial transcript exists and is in the Detroit Public Library (Burton Historical Collection).

[19] The text, along with a translation and some eight-five pages of notes, was printed by Patrick W. Browne as Volume I in the series *Studies in American Church History* published at The Catholic University of America (1922).

ment of the American Church was that of Father John Grassi, S.J. John Anthony Grassi was an Italian who came to this country in 1810 and for seven years played an intimate and great part in the expansion of the Church and of the Society of Jesus in America after its restoration. He was first assigned to Georgetown College and a year later made rector of that institution and superior of the Maryland mission. This office he kept until he returned to Europe in 1817. He wrote his memoir, *Notizie Varie*, in Milan, in the following year.[20]

The *Notizie Varie* is a book of 146 pages divided into three parts: notes on the climate, soil, products, commerce, population, characters, costume, literature and government (1–59); on the various sects in the states (60–110); and on the present state of the Catholic religion under two headings—" Dioceses " and " Churches and functions " (111–146). Annexed to the volume is a double page statistical table giving in parallel columns the names of states with latitude and longitude, area in square miles, products, minerals, population in 1790 and in 1810, inhabitants per square mile, capital and principal cities with respective population, universities and colleges, and a number of representatives in Congress. For historians the value of this comprehensive survey of American life lies chiefly in the fact that it presents a contemporary picture of the life of the missionaries of the time that can be found nowhere else. Grassi was writing for Europeans and naturally took a European viewpoint; he presented few new facts, but gave a valuable interpretation of his seven important years in this country.

---

[20] Giovanni Grassi, S.J., *Notizie varie sullo stato presente della Repubblica degli Stati Uniti d'America settentrionale, scritte al principio del 1818* (Milan, 1818). In 1819, a second edition was issued, a copy of which is in the Shea Collection in the Riggs Memorial Library at Georgetown University. A third edition was issued at Turin. Part of the work appeared in translation in the *American Catholic Historical Researches*, VIII (July, 1891), 98–111, taken from the *Woodstock Letters*, XI, No. 3. Another copy of the *Notizie varie* is in the possession of the American Catholic Historical Society of Philadelphia. Father Wilfrid Parsons, S.J., has made a worthwhile study of the volume in the *Catholic Historical Review*, V (January, 1920), 301–310.

The distinction of being the earliest history of the Catholic Church in the United States is usually assigned to *The Laity's Directory to the Church Service for the Year of Our Lord MDCCCXXII* (New York, 1822). It is a small volume of some 138 pages duodecimo and its compilation has been ascribed to the Reverend John Power, vicar-general of the diocese of New York. It is divided into eight sections, two of which, numbers four and five, bear directly on the subject of this essay; two others, numbers six and seven, are of somewhat less importance. The fourth section is captioned: " A Brief Account of the Establishment of Episcopacy in the United States " (72–80) ; section five has the title: " Present State of Religion in the Respective Dioceses " (18–121). Section six is " A Short Account, and Present State of the Society of Jesus in the United States " (122–126) ; section seven contains " Obituaries "—Archbishop Carroll, Francis Nagot, Archbishop Neale, Father Matignon and others (127–176).

The " Brief Account " consists mainly of the bull of Pius VI erecting the see of Baltimore, and a brief notice of the episcopal consecrations from John Carroll to John England. The section on the " Present State of Religion " has value chiefly because it lists the principal churches and the priests of each diocese. Unfortunately, its list of the priests in each diocese is not complete except the one for the diocese of New York. The information it gives, however, is accurate and was for many years the only reliable account of the status of the Church in that period.[21]

Almost a decade and a half elapsed before another description of the Church in the United States was attempted. In the year 1836, Bishop John England, of Charleston, wrote a brief but comprehensive account of the condition of the Church for the Central Council of the Society of the Propagation of the Faith, located at Lyons, France. Bishop England, at the request of the Council, undertook to answer four questions regarding the

---

[21] The " Brief Account " and the " Present State of Religion " were printed in the *Catholic Historical Review,* VI (October, 1920), 343–357. Few copies of this book are available.

Church in America. The answer, which came in the form of a letter, has six principal ideas.[22]

Bishop England's main thesis is that millions of the faithful had been lost to the Catholic religion in the United States during the fifty years since the establishment of the hierarchy. He explained that this loss was due to " the absence of a clergy sufficiently numerous and properly qualified for the missions of the United States." A second section is concerned with the methods employed by France and Spain in dealing with religion in their colonies in the New World. The third topic has to do with those portions of the country which from the beginning had been under Protestant domination, that is to say, the British colonies along the Atlantic Coast; here Bishop England gives a description of the condition of the few Catholics in these colonies before the American Revolution. England then treats the two colonies where the largest number of Catholics were to be found prior to the Revolution: Maryland and Pennsylvania. The fifth section deals with the expansion of the Church in the new Republic after the Treaty of Paris in 1783. The final section is concerned with the special difficulties facing the Church of that day, with particular emphasis on the evils of lay trusteeism.[23]

This letter of Bishop England was not his first attempt to describe the Church in America. In 1832, during a brief visit to Ireland, he printed in pamphlet form the early history of the diocese of Charleston including an account of his own work in the first twelve years of his episcopacy. In both of these historical narratives, England displays to advantage his keen powers of observation and analysis. Although there are many inaccuracies in the letter, the most notable being his estimate of the numerical loss the Church suffered in the brief span between 1785

---

[22] In the Reynolds edition of the *Works of John England* (Baltimore, 1849), this letter occupies twenty pages of closely printed text in double columns. The entire letter was first published in the *United States Catholic Miscellany,* (1839), Bishop England's official diocesan organ. It is reprinted in the Messmer edition of England's *Works* (Cleveland, 1908). The main portions of the letter were published first in the *Annales de la Propagation de la Foi,* I (March, 1838), No. 57.

[23] For an analysis of the letter cf. Peter Guilday, *Life and Times of John England: 1786–1842* (2 Vols., New York, 1927), II, 352–376.

to 1835, it must be remembered that England wrote it " from memory " while he was in Rome and without reference to notes or documents.  The historical value of the letter, however, does not rest on the statistical basis for England's assertion that the Church lòst 3,760,000 Catholics in the fifty years between 1785 to 1835, but rather on his vivid description of the causes for whatever leakage there may have been.  His account of the hindrances to Church progress will ever be of value to the historian of the American Church.[24]

There was an interlude of almost twenty years before another attempt was made to write a general history of the American Church.  In 1855, Thomas D'Arcy McGee published his *Catholic History of North America,* the first work at the hands of a Catholic claiming the title of history.

Thomas D'Arcy McGee was a fiery Irishman who came to America in 1842.  His whole life was one of movement and controversy.  A journalist by profession, he served on the staff of the *Boston Pilot* and soon became its editor-in-chief.  In 1845 he went back to Ireland where he soon became a leader in the Repeal agitation.  Three years later he was forced to quit Ireland, returning to America in the guise of a priest.  He started the *New York Nation,* which won recognition as one of the leading Irish organs in America.  McGee's criticism of the clergy and bishops of Ireland was answered in the press by Bishop John Hughes and as a result his influence began to wane rapidly, compelling him to remove to Boston.  Until 1850, when he founded the successful *American Celt,* his means of livelihood depended largely upon lectures he gave at private gatherings.  In 1857, he moved to Montreal and entered Canadian politics, becoming an ardent royalist.  He died at the hands of an assassin on April 7, 1868.[25]

The *Catholic History of North America* is a compilation of five

---

[24] The best study of Catholic leakage in the United States is Shaughnessy's *Has the Immigrant Kept the Faith?*  Bishop Shaughnessy based his study on all available sources, civil and ecclesiastical, and has shown how completely wide of the mark were England's figures.

[25] Cf. Isabel Skelton, *The Life of Thomas D'Arcy McGee* (Gardenvale, Canada, 1925), 161–162, 165–166.

of McGee's lectures delivered between 1854 and 1855 in New York, Boston, Philadelphia, Cincinnati, St. Louis and Washington. The book contains 239 octavo pages treating the following topics: (1) " Columbus and the Discovery; " (2) " The Successors of Columbus; " (3) " The Aborigines and the Missionaries; " (4) " The Catholics and the Revolution; " (5) " The Church in the Republic." Appended to the text are chapters on the " Relations of Ireland and America," " Historical Relations " and " Actual Relations " and " Documents Illustrative of the Catholic History of America." The documents given are: the will of Columbus; Letters and Bulls of Pope Alexander VI in relation to the discovery of America; Apostolic Letter of Pope Paul III, 1537, declaring the American Indians to be rational creatures; the Spanish form of taking possession of new territory; the Jesuits in Canada—a collection of extracts from Warburton's *Conquest of Canada;* address of the Roman Catholics of America to George Washington and his reply; an account of Catherine Tegakouita, illustrating the influence of Christianity on the domestic life of the Indians (taken from Bishop Kip's *Jesuits in America*).[26]

McGee has given in this compilation nothing better than a sketchy outline of the development of the Church in America. In the composition of the work he used second-hand sources exclusively and the few references he cites in the text are to well-known histories of the day. McGee wrote in a popular and journalistic style and the volume received widespread approval among Catholic readers, especially during the closing years of the Know-nothing movement. As a history of the Church in the United States, however, it is of very little importance.

Shortly after the publication of McGee's sketches came John Gilmary Shea's translation into English of a series of articles written by Henri de Courcy de Laroche Heron for the *Univers,* the *Ami de la Religion* and other French Catholic publications. Shea's translation was an octavo volume of 591 pages, printed at New York in 1856 and entitled: *The Catholic Church in the United States, a Sketch of Its Ecclesiastical History.* De Courcy

---

[26] *Ibid.,* 243–247.

was serving as an American correspondent for a number of French publications when he undertook to answer charges made against Archbishop Gaetano Bedini, apostolic visitor to the United States in 1853 and 1854. Archbishop Bedini's visit had caused. an outburst of anti-Catholic feeling which reached a climax in riots at Louisville and Cincinnati in 1853.[27]

After considerable correspondence with authorities in Bologna and Rome, De Courcy succeeded in obtaining some documentary materials for his purpose, but Archbishop Hughes, who was well aware of the growing anti-Catholic feeling through Know-nothingism, prevailed upon De Courcy not to publish the documents at that time. De Courcy then decided to publish in English his series of *Essais sur l'Histoire de la Religion Catholique des Etats Unis,* engaging John Gilmary Shea to assist him in the translation. Shea at the time was just beginning to make a reputation as an historian with the publication of his *Discovery and Exploration of the Mississippi Valley* and his *History of the Catholic Missions Among the Indian Tribes.* Shea generously put at De Courcy's disposal all the manuscripts, books and pamphlet materials he had collected. He then prepared a translation of the essays for the American public, owing, as he said, to " the want of any regular history of the Catholic Church in the United States." When the translation was finished, Shea went over the whole volume, adding paragraphs here and there, supplying references, and in some cases, writing new chapters for the book.[28] Since Shea had guided the writing of the articles in French by De Courcy, had then translated them into English, and had revised the whole from further sources at his disposal, the entire volume was largely his own.

The *Catholic Church in the United States,* which has since been known as the De Courcy-Shea *History,* purported to be a general history of the Catholic Church in America. As such, it remained but a skeleton until 1879 when Shea published a re-

---

[27] For Bedini cf. Peter Guilday, " Gaetano Bedini," *Historical Records and Studies,* XXIII (1933), 87–170.

[28] Peter Guilday, " John Gilmary Shea," *Historical Records and Studies,* XVII (1926), 45.

vised edition, bringing the narrative up to date and filling in many *lacunae* which had marred the 1856 edition. The first edition contains twenty-eight chapters, the first five of which deal successively with the early Indian missions; the colonial Church; the Church in the Republic; the Church in the Revolution; and a second chapter on the Church in the Republic. Chapters six to thirteen inclusive are concerned with the history of the diocese of Baltimore down to 1808, and of the archdiocese down to 1852. Chapters fourteen to eighteen inclusive cover the Church in Pennsylvania from 1680 to 1840; and chapters twenty to twenty-six are devoted to a study of the Church in New York. The last two chapters deal with the development of the anti-Catholic spirit which was so manifest in the colonial period and the rise of the Know-nothing movement. In the appendices, Shea prints thirty pages of documents relating to Bedini's rule in Bologna, previous to his visit to this country, the bull of Pius VI erecting the see of Baltimore and gives lists of prelates and priests in attendance at the Councils of Baltimore in 1791, 1829, 1837, 1840, 1843, 1846, 1849 and 1852; the marriage certificate of Jerome Bonaparte "as entered in the handwriting of Bishop Carroll" and a list of priests ordained in the dioceses of Baltimore, New York, Albany, Buffalo, Brooklyn and Newark.

Although free from too serious inaccuracies, the volume did not obtain the same acclaim as McGee's work. It received some severe criticism especially at the hands of Orestes Brownson, who cited it as "a series of newspaper articles, if we may so speak, on Church matters in the United States, hastily thrown off and carelessly strung together." [29]   That many of the harsh criticisms it received in the Catholic press were unjust can now be asserted. Limited as it was in point of time, the De Courcy-Shea *History* is a veritable treasure-trove for the research student. Its value to all writers in the field lies not only in the wide range of the sources it mentions, but in the variety of information it gives which cannot be obtained elsewhere.

The next important effort in the field of American Catholic Church history came in 1868 when the Reverend Charles Ignatius

---

[29] *Ibid.,* 46.

White, pastor of St. Matthew's Church, Washington, D. C., wrote a general account of the Church in America as an appendix to the English translation of Joseph E. Darras' *General History of the Catholic Church* (New York, 1866). Father White was a scholar of great erudition and " one of the outstanding literary figures in the American priesthood." [30]   His work in the field of journalism gained for him the reputation of being one of the leading publicists in the United States during the second half of the nineteenth century.   From 1834 to 1857, he edited under varying titles the *United States Catholic Almanac and Laity's Directory*.   In 1842, with the Reverend James Dolan, an early social worker in Baltimore, he founded and edited the *Religious Cabinet,* which was continued as the *United States Catholic Magazine* from 1843 to 1847.   In 1853 he founded and edited the *Metropolitan Magazine*.   Although these magazines compared favorably with contemporary secular publications, they were short-lived because of their erudite character.   In 1849 Father White assisted in founding the archdiocesan weekly paper, the *Catholic Mirror,* which he edited until 1855.   From 1837 until his death he assisted at all the Councils of Baltimore, provincial and plenary.   In the Councils of 1846, 1849, 1852 and 1866 he acted as theologian to Archbishops Eccleston, Kenrick and Spalding.[31] His ten years' service (1833–1843) in the cathedral at Baltimore as assistant and as rector allowed him opportunity for research into the diocesan archives ; and his intimate association with all the prelates and the leading priests of the country served to broaden his scholarly outlook.   Many years before he wrote the chapter on the Church in the United States for Darras' work, he had sufficiently demonstrated his ability as a critical historian by issuing a revised edition of J. L. Balmes' *Protestantism and Catholicity Compared in Their Effects on the Civilization of Europe* (Baltimore, 1850) and a *Life of Mrs. Eliza A. Seton, Foundress and First Superior of the Sisters of Charity in the United States* (New York, 1853), which later passed through several editions.

---

[30] Guilday, *England,* II, 551.

[31] English, *loc. cit.,* 588.   Cf. Richard J. Purcell, " Charles Ignatius White," *Dictionary of American Biography,* XX, 94–95.

With the assistance of Bernard U. Campbell, White collected a mass of source material for a projected sketch of the Church in the United States. Shea tells us that " he never actually wrote any part of his projected work, nothing having been found among his papers except a sketch of his plan." [32] The sketch actually written by White, and published in the last volume of the English translation of Darras, covers sixty-four pages and is entitled: " Sketch of the Origin and Progress of the Catholic Church in the United States of America." The sketch is marked off by Roman numerals into five sections of unequal length, yet covering the main divisions of American Church history. The first section is two and half pages of introduction; the second is ten pages covering the history from 1512 (the discovery of Florida) to 1791 (the enactment of the first ten amendments to the Constitution of the United States). The third division consists of twenty-five pages and treats the period from Carroll's consecration to the division of the diocese in 1808, while the fourth section brings the narrative down to the death of Archbishop Maréchal in 1828. The final division of fourteen pages completes the history to 1865 and includes a résumé of Catholic literature up to that time.

The work has few references but there is evidence that some original documents were used. Written in a journalistic style, it had its appeal for the general public but not the serious scholar. Because of the wide popularity it received, it did much to shape and color the Protestant mind for twenty-one years until the appearance of the monumental study by John Gilmary Shea. White's whole treatment of Carroll, says Guilday, " has given life to many legends about John Carroll which are still current in American Catholic circles." [33]

A little less than a decade after White's sketch there appeared what may be called the first general history of the Church in the United States. The new work was written by John O'Kane Murray, a practicing physician in Brooklyn, and published in 1876 under the title, *A Popular History of the Catholic Church in*

---

[32] English, *loc. cit.*, 588-589.
[33] Guilday, *Carroll*, 846.

*the United States.* A native of Ireland, Murray came to New York with his parents in 1856. He received his B.S. and M.A. degrees from St. John's College, Fordham, and later his medical degree from the University of the City of New York. He practiced medicine in New York until 1880, when he was stricken with tuberculosis. He then went to Chicago where he died on July 30, 1885. He was for a number of years a steady contributor to current Catholic periodicals, besides being the compiler of a number of books, the more notable of which were: *The Prose and Poetry of Ireland* (New York, 1877); *Catholic Heroes and Heroines of America* (New York, 1878); *Little Lives of the Great Saints* (New York, 1879); *Catholic Pioneers of America* (New York, 1881); and *Lessons in English Literature* (New York, 1883). Murray's *Popular History* was his first work and was written at the suggestion of Sadlier's publishing house for the approaching centennial celebration of Independence. Written at a time when there was a decided development in the scientific approach to history, Murray's book displays some signs of historical method. It is divided into six books. Books I and II are the general history of the Church in America; Books III to VI are its special history. Book I (1–162) carries the history from 1492 to 1775 in three chapters.[34] Book II (163–348) is divided into six chapters and takes the history down to 1876. Book III is devoted to the history of the religious orders, a chapter apiece to the orders of men (349–392) and the orders of women (393–424). Book IV covers in six chapters the field of Catholic education in the United States (425–481). Book V, likewise divided into six chapters (483–565), is concerned with Catholic literature in the United States, while Book VI is a treatment of the Irish contribution to America (566–578) and the problem of loss and gain in the American Church (579–604). At the end of each chapter there are appended a few biographies of the more important personages mentioned in the text, most of them prelates and priests, about one-fourth of the total being laymen.

Although the volume showed signs of the new scientific method,

---

[34] The pre-Columbian history is treated in four pages of the Appendix.

it was decidedly an inferior production, attracting little or no attention from the historical scholars of the period. Written in a journalistic style, it lived up to its title in every detail, and was uncommonly popular, reaching four editions within six months after its publication. It abounds in references to sources, some of which are now lost, but there are few signs of erudition. The topics treated in the appendices and notes are valuable as summaries of all that had been published up to that time on the question of Catholic literature in the United States and on the problem of loss and gain. The work as a whole displayed greater skill in arrangement than did the Shea translation of De Courcy. Although Murray frequently shows a dependence on the earlier works of Shea, his one volume contains many inaccuracies.

The period just surveyed, covering as it does one hundred years of Church history, displays, from the standpoint of modern critical historical scholarship, an inferior grade of historical writing on the American Church. Nowhere was this inferior order more noticeable than in the general histories of the Church. A certain amount of special history was appearing *pari passu,* which showed some evidence of historical method and was of a slightly higher order critically, such as White's *Life of Eliza A. Seton* and Sarah Brownson's *Life of Demetrius A. Gallitzin.* The period as a whole possessed no sense of historical judgment, no sense of historical reality, and little, if any, trace of critical reflection.

Shortly after the first quarter of the nineteenth century, however, one figure in the Church began to attract the attention of scholars by the results of his historical investigations. As early as 1838, the name of John Gilmary Shea was known to the public at large through his contributions to the *Catholic Magazine.* Described as the " American Bede " and the " Father of American Church History," he was the greatest historical scholar the American Church produced in the nineteenth century. In a survey of American Church historiography, he deserves a more detailed treatment than all the others, not only from the nature of his personal career and the influence he exerted on later Catholic writers, but also for the value of his contributions to systematic history and to the improvement of historical method.

# CHAPTER II

## John Gilmary Shea

John Gilmary Shea was born in New York on July 22, 1824, the son of James and Mary Ann (Flanigan) Shea. His father came from Ireland in 1815, and was prominent as a Tammany chieftain and a leader in Irish and Catholic affairs; he was an outstanding figure in the group that fought Bishops Dubois and Hughes on the trustee question. His mother traced her descent from Nicholas Upsall, one of Boston's earliest settlers, and from Thomas McCurtin, an Irish schoolmaster, who established a classical school at Mount Holly, New Jersey, in 1762.

Baptized John Dawson, Shea dropped his middle name and adopted Gilmary (Mary's servant) when he became a novice in the Society of Jesus.[1] The intellectual atmosphere of his early home must have influenced him unconsciously, but it does not seem likely that he owed directly to home influence any of the abiding interests and pursuits of his life. He received his early training in the Sisters of Charity school, in Mulberry Street, near the Cathedral, and in the Columbia Grammar School, graduating with honors in 1837. Frail in body and delicate in health, he had little capacity for organized sports; his gifts of mind naturally led him to reading and the study of nature. There is still among his papers a notebook entitled " John Dawson Shea's Herbarium for the years 1838, 1839, 1840," filled with well-preserved specimens of the rarer flowers that grew in and about New York. His searches were not confined to flowers, but to all sorts of mineral specimens; at home his " museum " was soon cluttered up with a variety of discoveries. It was at this time that he began his valuable collection of coins, and among his

---

[1] Guilday, " Shea," 15.  Cf. Richard J. Purcell, " John Dawson Gilmary Shea," *Dictionary of American Biography*, XVII, 50–52.

papers is a catalogue of the rare coins and medals he sent shortly before his death to the College of Mount Saint Vincent, New York.[2] It was during these years at school that Shea laid the foundations of that sound and accurate knowledge of linguistics which he possessed in later life. Although he never in any sense became a specialized linguistic scholar, he was never at a loss in translating many Indian dialects and most of the modern languages. Instead of continuing his studies at Columbia College, he procured through friendly connections a position in the commercial house of Don Thomas Stoughton, a Spanish merchant in the city.[3] It was his duty to meet the ships coming from Spanish ports to New York, to take care of the ship's papers and to assist the Spanish sailors in their purchases. With his unusual aptitude for languages, he quickly acquired a fluent knowledge of Spanish and wrote a biographical sketch of Alvarez Carrillo de Albornoz.[4] He soon tired of trade, however, and began the study of law which finally led to his being admitted to the bar in 1846. What his legal practice was for the next two years is uncertain, but there is evidence that he spent much of his time reading the sources for the colonial history of the Church in this country.

The two decades (1830-1850) were remarkable ones in the writing of American history. Scholars were aroused by the volumes published by Jared Sparks, Peter Force, George Bancroft and other writers whom John Spencer Bassett has placed in the middle group of American historians.[5] Fascinated by Bancroft's *History of the United States,* Shea became a member of the New York Historical Society, and wrote a series of nine articles on " Our Martyrs " for the *United States Catholic Magazine* in 1846–1847. These articles attracted attention, and many readers began to inquire about their author who had signed himself

---

[2] Guilday, " Shea," 16.

[3] For Don Thomas Stoughton, see William Harper Bennett, *Catholic Footsteps in Old New York* (New York, 1909), 391–394.

[4] Marc F. Vallette, " John Gilmary Shea," *The Catholic World,* LV (April, 1892), 56.

[5] John Spencer Bassett, *The Middle Group of American Historians* (New York, 1917).

" J.D.S." In the volume of the *Magazine* for 1848, Shea published other notices on Father Gabriel de la Ribourde, O.F.M., Fathers Du Poisson, Souel, and Senat, S.J., based on sources scarcely known to the Catholic literature of the day. These studies may well have been an important factor in the events which led him into the Society of Jesus in 1848. As a novice and scholastic he studied at St. John's College, Fordham, from 1848 to 1850, and at St. Mary's College, Montreal, from 1850 to 1852, where, in addition to attaining a fluent command of French, he acquired a sufficient knowledge of canon law to be consulted in later years by various prelates. Of more vital importance during these years was his close association with the trained Jesuit historian, Felix Martin, who at that time was a stimulating and helping force of great power. To Father Martin is due the accumulation of the rich store of documentary material for the study of New France, which he housed in the archives of St. Mary's College, Montreal, and from which John Gilmary Shea was later to draw the precious sources he published in his Cramoisy Series from 1857 to 1887. One of Shea's little-known works is his translation of Father Martin's *Life of Father Jogues* (New York, 1885). During this period of his scholastic development he also came under the influence of the historian of the State of New York, Edmund Bailey O'Callaghan.[6] For the next forty years, Shea's historical work was to follow closely the lines O'Callaghan had apparently projected for himself. The correspondence which passed between the two scholars reveals that O'Callaghan was at once an inspiration and model for America's foremost Catholic historian. That Shea did not become an historian of the Bancroft school can be largely attributed to O'Callaghan's influence. None of Bancroft's dramatic effect or lack of detachment can be discovered in the writings of Shea. His literary ability, like that of O'Callaghan, was to be subdued or, at least, to be kept in check by a passionate love of accuracy.

In June, 1852, Shea gave up thoughts of a religious life and

---

[6] Guilday, " Shea," 20–30. Cf. Francis Shaw Guy, *Edmund Bailey O'Callaghan, a Study in American Historiography; 1797–1880* (Washington, D. C., 1934), 51–55.

entered definitely on an historical career. In this same year he published his *Discovery and Exploration of the Mississippi Valley* which he dedicated to Jared Sparks. Guilday marks the publication of this work as the real beginning of his activity in the field of American Catholic historiography.[7] Before 1852 there was little of value to chronicle in this special field of American scholarship, and Shea's work won immediate success. The leading reviews of England and America welcomed it as one of the most noteworthy contributions to American history in recent years.[8] For the most part, the content of the book was made up of documents not accessible to scholars, and the critical notes appended to the text revealed an uncommon knowledge of colonial history. A volume of profound original research, it demonstrated Shea's capability in two different directions—that of exact, critical scholarship and that of lucid exposition.

The *Discovery and Exploration* contained the original narratives of Marquette, Allouez, Membré, Hennepin, and Anastase Douay, along with the Relation of Dablon and several unpublished documents relating to La Salle. It contained also the original map of the Marquette-Jolliet expedition of 1673, in Father Marquette's own handwriting. Apart from the critical notes in the text, Shea's contribution consists of a " Bibliographical Notice of Father Louis Hennepin," a " History of the Discovery of the Mississippi River," a " Life of Father Marquette " and a notice of " Sieur Jolliet." The work had an appeal for the scholar and collector, winning for Shea the favor of contemporary historians; and he received invitations to become a corresponding member of the historical societies of Wisconsin, Maryland, and Massachusetts, a rare honor for a Catholic during that period.

Meanwhile, Shea commenced to write many articles which appeared through succeeding years in the *United States Catholic Magazine,* the *Catholic World,* the *United States Historical Mag-*

---

[7] Guilday, " Shea," 35. It was Sparks who successfully urged Shea at the time to write the history of the early Catholic missions in Canada and the West. Cf. Michael Kraus, *A History of American History* (New York, 1937), 214.

[8] Guilday, " Shea," 36.

*azine,* the *American Catholic Quarterly Review,* the *Boston Pilot,* and other publications. While a few of these contributions were of a critical and learned nature, most of them were popular. However, they were on the whole far better than the ordinary article of the same type, and added to Shea's reputation.

During the two years following his stay in Montreal, Shea was a frequent guest in social circles and a familiar figure at meetings where the cause of Irish freedom was discussed. It was at this time he met and married Miss Sophie Savage, of old Puritan lineage. The marriage proved to be happy in every respect. During the forty years of their married ilfe, Mrs. Shea's co-operation was unfailing, and their two daughters, Ida and Emma Isabel, were trained by her to be competent aids to their father in his varied activities. Family responsibility compelled Shea to form a connection with the publishing firm of E. Dunigan and Brother. In quick succession he compiled for this house a *First Book of History* (New York, 1854), a *General History of Modern Europe* (New York, 1854) and a *School History of the United States* (New York, 1855), which was adopted rather widely in Catholic schools. Other signs of the financial pressure Shea experienced during these years are his works published by D. and J. Sadlier, including an *Elementary History of the United States* (New York, 1855) and *The Catholic Church in the United States: a Sketch of Its Ecclesiastical History* (New York, 1856), the translation of the work of Henri DeCourcy, revised and enlarged in 1879.[9] Shea found time to carry on many varied activities: to contribute several chapters to Justin Winsor's *Narrative and Critical History of America;* to compile articles for encyclopedias; to edit Sadlier's *General Catholic Directory* from 1858 to 1890; to assist James Lenox in collecting Americana; to serve Archbishop Hughes as a diocesan historiographer, with a resultant volume, *The Catholic Churches of New York City* (New York, 1878) ; to edit the *Library of American Linguistics* from 1860 to 1874, including some fifteen Indian grammars and dictionaries; to help edit the *Historical Magazine* from 1855 to 1867; to edit without credit a pocket *Catholic Bible* and a patriotic

---

[9] See p. 14.

volume of sketches, *Fallen Brave: A Biographical Memorial of the American Officers Who Have Given Their Lives for the Preservation of the Union* (New York, 1861) ; and to join Bishop John Ireland, R. H. Clarke, and Charles G. Herbermann in founding the United States Catholic Historical Society, of which he was elected president in 1890 and editor of its publications from 1887 to 1889.[10]

Despite these many enterprises, he continued to work in his own field, compiling in 1854 the *History of the Catholic Missions Among the Indian Tribes of the United States: 1529–1854.* The volume was the result of ten years spent in collecting materials and historical research and was certainly the most valuable volume on this subject that had issued from the American Catholic press up to that time. Shea's labor on this book was considerable, for the sources he uses make up a creditable library of early Americana. Even Orestes Brownson, who was prone to disparage any glory given to the French Catholic missionaries, admitted that the book was " a work of solid merit, entitling the author to an honorable rank among our historical writers." [11] Writers such as Bancroft, Sparks, O'Callaghan and Kip had not stinted their praise in dealing with the Catholic missionaries and had given them a merited place in the country's history. Shea, however, wished to show that the result of the labors of the missionaries was a permanent one, and that to deny them any lasting success was an unfair use of historical criticism. Shea writes:

> The great decrease of the Indians may indeed in part excuse some writers from not knowing the real state of little communities, now hemmed-in by the busy whites; and it would excuse them, were it not very evident that they decide the results of the missions, not from observation, but from preconceived ideas of the Catholic Church. One remarkable fact will, at all events, appear in the course of this work, that the tribes evangelized by the French and Spaniards subsist to this day, except where brought in contact with the colonists of

---

[10] See pp. 43–45.
[11] Guilday, " Shea," 38.

England and their allies or descendants; while it is no-
torious that the tribes in the territory colonized by England, have in many cases entirely disappeared, and
perished without ever having had the gospel preached to
them. The Abnakis, Caughnawagas, Kaskaskias, Mi-
amis, Ottawas, Chippeways, Arkansas, and the New
Mexican tribes remain, and number faithful Christians;
but where are the Pequods, Narragansetts, the Mo-
hegans, the Mattowax, the Lenape, the Powhatans?
They live only in name in the rivers and mountains of
our land.[12]

For the first time we get a glimpse at Shea's historical spirit
in the Preface of the volume. He says:

In writing I have endeavored to be just to all men, to
avoid all partiality, to take no part in the rivalries wh:ch
have existed and still exist, all tending to overshadow
the truth, and give theories or party views for a real
picture. of the historical facts.[13]

There was a charm and eloquence about the *History of the
Catholic Missions* which attracted all who read it, and edition
followed edition in rapid succession until the War between the
States. Shea's dramatic description of what Catholic priests had
undergone to plant the seeds of the faith in the New World
brought out in clear relief the legacy the missionaries of old had
bequeathed to the generation of Catholics for whom he was writing; and in more than one place his pages awakened the pertinent
question: what was the Catholic Church in the United States
doing to preserve the faith among the Catholic Indian tribes
which had survived the white man's conquest of the West?

The historical and literary work of John Gilmary Shea during
the quarter of a century from 1857 to 1882 may be regarded from
various points of view. During these years he belonged by right
of his profound scholarship and his numerous publications to
that small group of outstanding American historians who were

---

[12] *History of the Catholic Missions among the Indian Tribes of the
United States: 1529–1854* (New York, 1883), 15–16.
[13] *Ibid.*, 17.

writing between Prescott's death in 1859 and Bancroft's passing 1891—George Ticknor (1791–1871), Henry C. Lea (1825–1907), John Lothrop Motley (1814–1877), and Francis Parkman (1823–1893). In point of numbers, Shea's publications outstrip those of almost all his contemporaries; close to one hundred volumes, besides a long list of periodical articles came from his pen during the years under review.

When in the Jesuit novitiate, Shea had read and studied the precious collections of original manuscripts which Father Felix Martin was assembling in the archives of St. Mary's College, Montreal. Urged by Dr. O'Callaghan to publish these sources, Shea made several attempts to persuade Martin to lend him a number of the *Relations*. Finally, the Society of Jesus gave Shea the required permission to issue a series of reprints of these rare sources. These manuscripts consisted of written accounts of the labors of the Jesuit missionaries in North America, which it was their duty to send each year to their superior in Montreal. At the end of each year, the Jesuit superior sent to the superior in Paris a redaction of the letters he had received. This summary was called a Relation, and was a narrative of the most important events occurring in the district under his care. Between 1623 and 1673, these narratives were carefully edited by the French superior and were then published from the press of Sebastian Cramoisy. Forty volumes in all were issued and were well received in educated circles. With the succeeding years The Cramoisys, as they were called, became rare, and, when O'Callaghan called attention to them in his *Jesuit Relations* (1847), no complete set was known to exist in America. With the assistance of O'Callaghan and Shea, James Lenox began to collect these rare volumes, and today what is probably the only complete set of Cramoisys is in the Lenox Library in New York. In 1858, the Canadian government reprinted the Cramoisys in three large octavo volumes which are now so scarce that copies are seldom offered for sale.

Shea began the publication of these manuscripts in 1857 and for a period of thirty years the booklets were issued to a chosen number of friends and historical students. One hundred copies were printed of the two editions which appeared (one in octavo and the other in duodecimo) and are now among the *rarissima* of our American libraries.

The Cramoisy Series has been unevenly estimated by historical scholars. The fact that Shea did call attention to the *Relations* as of prime importance for the student of French colonial America won him a unique place in American historiography. Yet the series as a whole left a sense of dissatisfaction in the mind of almost every careful reader because of the poor printing and the unsatisfactory juxtaposition of the materials which the printer arranged to his own satisfaction.

In 1865, Shea began work on a translation of Father F. X. de Charlevoix' *History and General Description of New France,* which he published in six volumes between 1866 and 1872. For this scholarly effort, Shea received high praise. One reviewer wrote:

> The spirit and the manner in which Mr. Shea has entered upon his task are above all praise. It is with him a " labor of love." In these days of literary " jobs " when bad translating and careless editing are palmed off on the amateurs of choice books in all the finery of broad margins and faultless typography, it is refreshing to meet with a book of which the mechanical excellence is fully equalled by the substantial value of its contents, and by the thorough, conscientious and scholar-like character of the literary execution. The labor and the knowledge bestowed on this translation would have sufficed to produce an original history of high merit. Charlevoix rarely gives his authorities. Mr. Shea has more than supplied the deficiency. Not only has he traced out the sources of his author's statements and exhibited them in notes, but he has had recourse to sources of which Charlevoix knew nothing. He is thus enabled to substantiate, correct or amplify the original narrative. He translates it, indeed, with literal precision, but in his copious notes he sheds such a flood of new light upon it that this translation is of far more value to the student than the original work. Since Charlevoix's time, many documents unknown to him, though bearing on his subject, have been discovered, and Mr. Shea has

diligently availed himself of them. The tastes and studies of many years have made him familiar with this field of research, and prepared him to accomplish an undertaking which would otherwise have been impracticable.[14]

The translation filled a gap in the historical literature of America. The edition was limited to two hundred and fifty copies on large paper and forty on small paper; the large edition sold for twelve dollars a volume and the small one for half that price.

For a period of six years, 1876–1882, Shea worked assiduously among his papers and documents, putting all his sources in order and projecting his *History of the Catholic Church in the United States*. As early as September, 1876, he had asked Archbishop Bayley of Baltimore for a letter of recommendation to all who possessed archival material for his purpose. The archbishop's letter did much to encourage Shea and opened to him many archives here and abroad. Shea refused at this time to listen to the suggestion of Bishop Richard Gilmour of Cleveland that he give up all other tasks and become the official historiographer of the Church in the United States. He was too diffident about his ability to satisfy the hierarchy in so important a work and preferred to carry it through in a private capacity.

In the years 1882–1883, Shea began the preparation of the first volume of his monumental, critical, and impartial history of the Catholic Church in the United States. The volume was to cover the years 1521 to 1763 and was to have the title: *The Catholic Church in Colonial Days—The Thirteen Colonies—The Ottawa and Illinois Country—Louisiana—Florida, Texas—New Mexico and Arizona.* His previous research of over forty years had furnished him with first-hand material for this first section of the history, but he hesitated to begin its actual composition. The first problem was to fill up whatever gaps there were in his material. He possessed at this time a library of over twenty thousand books, pamphlets, and manuscripts of which he had in many instances the only known copy. To complete this source material, he began a correspondence which included scholars of

---

[14] Cf. Guilday, " Shea," 70.

all countries. His letters to members of the American hierarchy aroused a national interest, and when the prelates met at the Third Plenary Council of Baltimore in November-December, 1884, a committee consisting of four archbishops was appointed to co-operate with Shea in the publication of this important work.[15]   It was while attending the closing public sessions of this Council of Baltimore that the same group of prelates met him for the purpose of discussing a complete history of the Catholic Church in this country.   The first centenary of the establishment of the see of Baltimore was near at hand (1889), and it was the opinion of all that the time was opportune for a scholarly review of the hundred years that had passed.   Shea returned from the Council with the assurance that the work would be supported; he saw in prospect the fulfillment of his life's dream.   There was no lack of encouragement.   Cardinal Gibbons was a constant source of support to the venerable historian, and the letters which passed between them reveal a little known side of Gibbons' historical interest.   Second only to that of Cardinal Gibbons was the support of Archbishop Michael A. Corrigan of New York. Around him was a small group of priests and laymen whose interest in Shea's project was as keen as his own.   Among these were: Monsignori Quinn, Preston and Edwards of New York, Father John M. Farley, who succeeded Corrigan in 1902 and became the second cardinal of New York in 1911; Reverend Patrick Corrigan of Hoboken; and Eugene Kelly, William R. Grace, and many others.[16]       .

The first volume of the *History* was ready in the closing months of 1886.   Issued under the title: *The Catholic Church in Colonial Days: 1521–1763*, the work is divided into four books, each of which is subdivided into three parts: the Catholic Church in the English, Spanish, and French colonies or territories respectively.   In reality the volume is made up of three sections devoted to the three chief colonizing nations, England, Spain, and France, with two chronological divisions common to the three sections: 1500–1690; 1690–1763.   This plan, confusing

[15] *Ibid.*, 95.
[16] *Ibid.*, 100.

as it is, was the only logical method of treating in a general way so large a subject. The welcome the book received on its appearance removed all doubt from Shea's mind. It was recognized by all as a splendid achievement.

Two years crowded with many anxieties, financial and family troubles, and his own fitful spells of exhaustion, were to intervene before the next volume, *The Life and Times of Archbishop Carroll* was ready for the press. The second volume proved to be even more successful than the first. The times were almost within the memory of many who were still living and at that time the name of John Carroll loomed up in the Catholic life of the United States as did that of George Washington in its political history. The *Life and Times of Archbishop Carroll* runs along more smoothly than the first volume since the chronology is without a break. There is a charm about the style that betrays how near its author had come to the heart of the Father of the American Hierarchy. Shea had rescued from oblivion hundreds of facts which enhanced the renown of John Carroll among Americans generally, and among these facts was Carroll's part in the founding of Georgetown College. The centenary of the school came that year, and early in January Shea received a letter from Father J. Havens Richards, S.J., then President of Georgetown University, informing him that the authorities had decided to confer upon him a medal in honor of his *Life and Times of Archbishop Carroll* and suggesting that he write a centenary history of Georgetown College. Shea accepted and the history of the College appeared in 1891.

Increased financial difficulties and failing health, brought on by a strain of the ligaments of his left leg and from which he never fully recovered, delayed the appearance of the third volume of the *History* until February, 1891. In the meantime, Shea wrote to Archbishop Corrigan in 1889, asking for a clerkship in the chancery office or even in Calvary Cemetery in order to relieve his impoverishment. When the Catholic University of America was established at Washington, D. C., he hoped for a call to the chair of history, but in this he was bitterly disappointed. Instead he was given the editorship of the *Catholic News* of New York City which enabled him to support his family in Elizabeth, New Jersey, and to finish the *History*. The third volume is divided into six books. The first book treats of the province of Baltimore from 1815 to 1829. Book two deals with the dioceses of Louisiana and the Floridas, New Orleans, St. Louis and the vicariate of Alabama. Book three consists of two chapters on the First Provincial Council of Baltimore, and the growth of anti-Catholic feeling. Book four returns to the province of Baltimore and gives the history of that archdiocese and of its suffragan sees from 1829 to 1843. The fifth book returns to the Middle West and Louisiana, and the last book treats of Texas. The arrangement is unsatisfactory and gives the impression of notes hastily put together in a geographical classification and then strung together in a unit. The whole of the United States at the time still comprised one ecclesiastical province, that of Baltimore, and the work would have perhaps gained in strength and clarity had Shea followed a less rigid outline. Nothing of importance is missing, however. Every detail of Catholic life during these stirring years is told, and the volume, like all of Shea's work, is a mine for the research student.

During the summer of 1891, Shea laid aside his work on the *History* because of ill health. Realizing that he did not have many more years to live, he was determined to finish the *History* before his death. Resuming work in the fall of 1891, he labored with the consciousness that every hour counted and that it was to be a race to the end. However, Shea did not live to see the publication of the fourth and final volume of his monumental work. Taken with a chill on February 13, 1892, while going over the proof sheets of the last volume, he never recovered sufficiently to resume his work. He died on February 22. The final volume was published by Mrs. Shea in the course of the year, and was dedicated to Father Patrick Corrigan, whose interest in the work and whose generous support had lightened the last three years of Shea's life. No preface appeared in the volume, since he did not have time to write one, and so the intimate insight he usually gave to the problems connected with his researches and labors is missing.

The fourth volume covers the period of a prodigious stride of the Catholic Church in the United States, from the Fifth Provincial Council of Baltimore to the Second Plenary Council (1843–1866). There are thirteen books, each divided into chapters following approximately the geographical growth of the Church in this country. As in his earlier volumes, illustrations abound and his pages are replete with maps, portraits of bishops and priests, illustrations of old churches and institutions, and with facsimiles of episcopal seals and signatures—all chosen with that rare judgment and taste which he displayed in all his historical writings.

As a history of the years 1521–1866, Shea's *History of the Catholic Church in the United States* can hardly be superseded. All who write within the field must turn to his volumes as to the principal source of their researches. His scholarship is evident on every page. His style is eloquent and persuasive; and there is an earnestness about his treatment of every point under consideration which leaves no room for doubt as to his irreproachable sincerity and zeal for the truth. Shea's sense of fairness has been questioned on only one score: his admiration for the work of the Society of Jesus. After a most careful examination of the *History,* however, it has been shown that the objection is groundless.[17] Another objection made against Shea touches a less serious aspect of his scholarship. With the exception of his *Life and Times of Archbishop Carroll,* the history is lacking in symmetry; and with another notable exception—*The Catholic Missions*—this is true of all his historical volumes. The first, third, and fourth volumes of the *History of the Church in the United States,* while well-written, are, it is true, constructed unsatisfactorily. The order of time is naturally kept in each section and chapter and book of these volumes, but the arrangement of each volume leaves much to be desired. The problem of treating in a systematic fashion geographical units that will stand apart ecclesiastically in spite of all identities and similarities was too much for Shea and has yet to be solved.

To construct an estimate of John Gilmary Shea's historical works as a whole is not an easy task. They consist of so many varied aspects of the historical sciences: linguistics, philology,

---

[17] *Ibid.,* 149–151.

paleography, historical geography and chronology, the ethnology of the American Indians, critical editions of original texts, biographies, treatises on general historical subjects, his biblical studies, his contributions to encyclopedias and periodical reviews, that a composite analysis is hazardous. Shea had all the essential qualities of a self-trained scholar and for the most part developed them without aid. When the comparative insufficiency of his actual training is remembered, the mastery he achieved in the realm of history is as remarkable as it is admirable.

As the greatest American Catholic historical writer, Shea received little contemporary appreciation for his work. Catholic colleges were not teaching history except as a stilted drill in questions and answers. The study of American history was not recognized; the hierarchy was more interested in building churches and charitable institutions than in records and historical scholarship. But the Catholic Church in America owes to John Gilmary Shea a debt that can never be substantially repaid as Monsignor Guilday has written:

> In Shea's life, in the recital of the many difficulties which he carried on his great work, in the tragic poverty that was ever present all through his years almost until the end, and in the unselfish and uncomplaining way he worked out his self-appointed task, the aspirants of our day have an exemplar unique in the annals of lay apostleship. Wherever his memory is cherished as one who gave of his rich and mature scholarship to the Catholic Church in the United States, there will his zeal find an emulation; and his example a worthy following.[18]

---

[18] *Ibid.*, 154.

# CHAPTER III

## Catholic Historical Societies

In the middle of the nineteenth century, when the strict methods of procedure in other sciences were applied to history and gave rise to the science of historical research and historical criticism, this science brought with it scholarly co-operation on an international scale. National historical societies were formed to act as clearing-houses for historical investigation and controversy. Historical journals, with all their scientific apparatus of notes and references, were created to give publicity to existing research and to provide reviews of current historical literature.[1]

The growth of historical societies and historical journals in the United States was prodigious. By the beginning of the twentieth century, approximately five hundred voluntary societies devoted to historical research and study were in existence in this country, giving it high rank among the nations of the world.[2]

In 1883 Pope Leo XIII created widespread interest in the field of church history by opening the archives of the Vatican to the scholars of the world. In his letter *Saepenumero considerantes* of August 18, 1883, addressed to Cardinals Antonine de Luca, John Baptist Pitra, librarian of the Vatican, and Joseph Hergenröther, prefect of the Vatican Archives, the Pope enlisted scholars the world over to defend the Church against the attacks

---

[1] In the field of ecclesiastical history a remarkable number of scholarly journals made their appearance in Europe, a few of which were: *Revue d'Histoire ecclésiastique* (Louvain, 1900); *Études* (Paris, 1856); *Revue des Questions historiques* (Paris, 1866); *Bulletin d'ancienne Littérature et d'Archéologie chrétienne* (Paris, 1911); *Analecta Bollandiana* (Brussels, 1882); *Revue Bénédictine* (Maredsous, 1884); *Archivum Franciscanum historicum* (Quaracchi, 1908); *Revue Mabillon* (Paris, 1905) and *Nederlandsch Archief voor Kerkgeschiedenis* (The Hague, 1884).

[2] Cf. Waldo G. Leland, "Concerning Catholic Historical Societies," *Catholic Historical Review*, II (January, 1917), 389.

of those who were using falsified history as their chief weapon.[3]

Catholic scholars in the United States were not slow to respond to the trend. Pope Leo's letter and the appeal for historical study sent out to Catholic America by the assembled prelates at the Third Plenary Council of Baltimore in 1884 gave added incentive to the movement already under-way. There began almost immediately an exceptional growth in the number of Catholic historical societies and historical reviews to promote a wider and deeper study of the Church in America. As a result the Catholic Church became better represented in this field than all the other religious bodies taken together.[4] "American Catholics," writes Leland, "have done more for their history than have any of the Protestant denominations."[5] In the last half century, these American Catholic historical societies have been particularly fruitful and the activities of their members have played a prominent rôle in the advance of the scientific method and the diffusion of historical knowledge about the past of the Catholic Church.

An immediate and significant response to Pope Leo's appeal to historical scholars was made by one who had been pioneering for a number of years in historical research in the Ohio Valley. As early as May, 1879, Andrew Arnold Lambing had attempted to organize a Catholic historical society in Pittsburgh for the purpose of collecting all the data extant in that locality on the Church, but the plan did not succeed.[6] Realizing, as did many historical scholars of that period, that too little interest was being

---

[3] This letter can be found in the original Latin in Stang's *Historiographia Ecclesiastica* (Louvain, 1897) ; in translation in the London *Tablet*, LXII (September 1, 1883), 321–323, and in the *Ave Maria*, XIX (1883), 741–743, 761–763. The Pope's mind on the matter of historical studies is more fully portrayed if we supplement this letter by his letter to the archbishop of Vienna, excerpts from which can be found in the London *Tablet*, LXII (September 22, 1883), 441, 444, as well as the encyclical letter to the French clergy in the London *Tablet*, XCIV (September 23, 1899), 497–499.

[4] Cf. A. P. C. Griffin, "Bibliography of American Historical Societies," American Historical Association *Annual Report*, II, 1905 (Washington, D. C., 1907).

[5] *Loc. cit.*, 390.

[6] "The Story of a Failure: The Ohio Valley Catholic Historical Society," *Catholic Historical Review*, I (January, 1916), 435–438.

manifested by American Catholics in collecting and preserving the records of the past, Lambing, with a few friends, founded in February, 1884, the first organization for this purpose in the United States, the Ohio Valley Catholic Historical Society.[7] This second venture of Father Lambing to found a Catholic historical society did not live long, several causes contributing to its failure:

> The city of Pittsburgh and the surrounding district at this time resembled a vast workshop, and there were very few scholars in and around the town who were in-interested in the historical past of their vicinity. The number of wealthy and influential Catholics was so small, and even those who could have supported the society were too engrossed in the industrial progress of Pittsburgh to take much interest in historical pursuits. The clergy and the diocesan authorities were equally uninterested. Most of them had come from abroad and their interest lay in other countries.[8]

In 1879 the older citizens of Pittsburgh formed the Old Residents' Association of Pittsburgh and Western Pennsylvania which later branched out into the Historical Society of Western Pennsylvania. When this occurred, the Ohio Valley Catholic Historical Society dissolved, having met only a few times, and Father Lambing became a prominent member of the non-Catholic organization, presiding for a long term of years as president. In July, 1884, Lambing began, as a private venture, the publication of a small quarterly magazine called *Historical Researches in Western Pennsylvania Principally Catholic,* which title he later changed to *Catholic Historical Researches.* In December, 1886, the quarterly was transferred to Martin I. J. Griffin of Philadelphia who published it until his death in 1911 under the title *American Catholic Historical Researches.* After Griffin's death, the journal continued to appear under the editorship of William L. J Griffin until the end of the twenty-ninth volume in July,

---

[7] Two months later he instituted the first diocesan historical library in the United States, when he formed the Historical Library of the Diocese of Pittsburgh.

[8] " The Story of a Failure," *loc. cit.,* 438.

1912, when it combined with the *Records* of the American Catholic Historical Society of Philadelphia. The first issue of the joint periodical appeared in September, 1912.

Although Lambing did not originally intend to confine himself to Western Pennsylvania and the valley of the Ohio, these sections dominate the papers published between July, 1884, and October, 1886.[9] The *Researches* under the direction of Martin I.

---

[9] These volumes are among the *rarissima* of Catholic Americana and their contents deserve to be noted here. The articles in Volume I are: "Celoron's Expedition down the Allegheny and Ohio Rivers, 1749," 1–31; "The Early Days of Catholicity in Pittsburgh," 32–36; "Historical Library of the Catholic Diocese of Pittsburgh," 37–40; "The First Printing Press in New World," 40; "The French in Western Pennsylvania in Early Times," 41–58; "Register of the Baptisms and Interments Which Took Place at Fort Duquesne during the Years 1753–1756," 60–73; "The Early Days of Catholicity in Pittsburgh," 76–80; "Points on the Early History of Pittsburgh," 81–98; "The Acadians in Philadelphia," 98–102; Register of the Baptisms and Interments Which Took Place at Fort Duquesne during the Year 1753–1756," 102–118; "The Establishment of the Catholic Hierarchy in the United States," 121–136; "Did LaSalle Descend the Allegheny and Ohio Rivers, 1669–1670?" 137; "Register of the Baptisms and Interments Which Took Place at Fort Duquesne during the Years 1753–1756," 138–154; "The Early Days of Catholicity in Pittsburgh," 154–160. Volume II, known as the *Catholic Historical Researches,* contained the following: "The Establishment of the See of Pittsburgh," 3–14; "First See and Bishop on the American Continent," 14–16; "Register of the Baptisms and Interments Which Took Place at Fort Duquesne during the Years 1753–1756," 18–25; "Notes, Original Documents, etc.," 25–32; "Washington and the Catholics of the United States," 32–35; "The Ohio Valley Catholic Historical Society of Pittsburgh," 38–39; "The American Catholic Historical Society of Philadelphia," 39–40; "The United States Catholic Historical Society of New York," 40; "Supposed Vestiges of Early Christian Teaching in the New World," 41–54; "Gibault, the Patriot Priest," 54–60; "Celoron's Journal," 60–76; "The Site of Fort Duquesne," 77; "Notes, Original Documents, etc.," 78–80; "New Hampshire Intolerance," 81–88; "Necrology of the Diocese of Pittsburgh," 88–102 (the volume is here annotated with numerous lead-pencil and pen corrections in the handwriting of Griffin); "Celoron's Journal," 103–119; "The Constitution of the United States and Religious Liberty," 121–131; "Celoron's Journal," 132–146; "Some Vicars-General of Philadelphia" (Middleton), 146–147; "A Century of Catholicity in Green County, Pennsylvania," 148–153. Volume III contains: "Stephen Badin, the

J. Griffin maintained the relatively high standard which had been set by the earlier publication. An indefatigable delver, Griffin collected and printed in the *Researches* a large amount of original and secondary data of great assistance to the historian of the development of the Church in the United States.[10]

The year 1884 was one of great moment in the historiography of the American Church, witnessing as it did the foundation of three Catholic historical societies; two of these, in the years following, destined to develop gradually and become in our own day worthy of being ranked with the few leading historical societies in the country.

A series of conversations during the summer of 1884, on the subject of Catholic history between Martin I. J. Griffin, John H. Campbell and William J. Campbell, eventually led to the foundation of the American Catholic Historical Society of Philadelphia on July 12 of that year. These men met with some able laymen and priests in the Catholic Temperance Hall in Philadelphia and formulated the plans for the society. The organization of the society was completed at a meeting held December 10, 1884, when Father Thomas Cooke Middleton, O.S.A., was chosen its first president.[11] The aims of the new society were to collect, preserve and publish all documentary material relating to the history

Proto-priest of the United States," 1–13; "Andrew White, S.J., the Apostle of Maryland," 13–20; "Detroit in Early Times—Gabriel Richard," 41–58; "Gallitzin," 58–68; "The Famous Bull of Pope Alexander VI" (Latin and English), 71–79.

[10] Although the contents of the *Researches* can be grouped under three broad headings: 1) historical compositions on almost any phase of American Catholic history; 2) transcripts of Church registers and records; and 3) letters of bishops, priests and prominent Catholic laymen, the amount of the material published in the twenty-nine volumes is too voluminous to be analyzed here. Most of the worthwhile material has been used and cited by many of the leading historians in the field and is, therefore, more or less well-known. To facilitate research, however, the *Researches* is adequately indexed from the initial issue in July, 1884, until 1912 when it was merged with the *Records*.

[11] "Golden Jubilee of the American Catholic Historical Society, 1884–1934," *Records of the American Catholic Historical Society*, XLV (1934), 193–194. (Hereinafter cited as *Records*.)

of the Church in America, to investigate the origin and progress of Catholicism in the United States, to form a national Catholic historical library and archives, and to encourage interest in Catholic history in general.[12] How faithful the society has been in carrying out its aims can be readily seen by reviewing some of its accomplishments during the past sixty years. Two years after its formation, the society began the publication of a quarterly journal known as the *Records of the American Catholic Historical Society*. In the fifty-three volumes of the *Records* that have been published to date, the research student will find a host of scholarly articles, reprints and original sources for Catholicism's rise and advance in every part of the country. The *Records* have not only made available a mass of information referring to many old families, who took an active part in the planting of the Catholic faith in the New World, but also indicated the sources for further research. It has published a remarkable number of excellent essays on the beginnings of local Catholic history, the experiences of missionaries, and the rise and development of Know-nothingism in various states. There are in its pages many valuable accounts of parish histories for some of the old Catholic centers in New York, New Jersey, Pennsylvania, Delaware, Ohio and Maryland. One of the outstanding accomplishments of the periodical is the number of original documents it has managed to collect and publish. Chief among these are the documents from the Baltimore Cathedral Archives and the Archiepiscopal Archives of Quebec, bearing not only on the Church in Baltimore and Philadelphia but also in the Mississippi Valley. Of special importance are the documents dealing with the erection of the see of Baltimore and the appointment of its first bishop. The other documents include the registers of baptisms, marriages and funerals in some of the old churches, letters of private and official correspondence, diaries, deeds, wills, charters, and the minutes of old Church corporations. Among the important diaries it reproduces are those of Bishop England; Patrick Kenny, the mis-

---

[12] "Charter of the American Catholic Historical Society of Philadelphia," *Records*, I (1884–1886), 6–8. Cf. Peter Guilday, "Quadraginta Annis: 1884–1924," *Records*, XXXVII (1926), 1–22.

sionary priest of Delaware and the southeastern counties of Pennsylvania from 1804 until the time of his death in 1840; Bishop Flaget and that of Venerable Bishop Neumann. Each volume of the *Records* is indexed. A separate index of over five hundred pages has been issued for the first thirty-one volumes.

After John Gilmary Shea had revealed in his *History of the Catholic Church in the United States* the rich sources for American Catholic history in foreign archives, the society began planning the establishment of archivists in all the large centers of Europe and America where documents existed. The society sent Father Ferdinand Kittell as its archivist to Rome, where he copied documents in the Vatican and Propaganda archives and made a transcription of all the American letters in the portfolios of the Irish College in Rome. Many of these transcripts were later printed in the *Records*.[13] When the society had to abandon these ambitious projects because of lack of funds, it continued to receive valuable transcripts from the noted historian, Monsignor Umberto Benigni.

The library and museum of the society have become a regular treasure-trove of Catholic Americana. The library and cabinet contain over 40,000 volumes, not including bound files of newspapers, and close to 10,000 manuscripts, mostly letters. The collection excels in Catholic newspapers, rare pamphlets, sermons, lectures and biographical sketches. It includes the library and some personal belongings of the Reverend Demetrius A. Gallitzin (1779–1840) ; Catholic Directories from 1822; early copies of the *Catholic Herald* of Philadelphia (1833–1846) ; the diary of Bishop John Neumann (1852–1860) ; miters, vestments, chalices and monstrances. This *monumenta* of history and religion was until recent years located at the residence of the society at 715 Spruce Street, Philadelphia. It is now housed at the Seminary of St. Charles Borromeo, Overbrook, Pennsylvania. The con-

---

[13] " Papers relating to the Church in America, from the Portfolios of the Irish College at Rome," *Records,* VII (1896), 283–388, 454–492; VIII (1897), 195–240, 294–329, 450–512; IX (1898), 1–34.

tents of the library and museum have been described in the *Records*.[14]

On December 9, 1884, two days after the closing of the Third Plenary Council of Baltimore, John Gilmary Shea and Richard H. Clarke met with a group of prominent men in the office of the Catholic Protectory in New York City and founded the United States Catholic Historical Society. The society was an outgrowth of the Council of Baltimore. The impression of those present at this first meeting was that the bishops, notably Cardinal McCloskey and Archbishop Corrigan, had inspired the project.[15] Among those taking an active part in its formation besides Shea and Clarke were Bishop John Ireland, Reverend R. L. Burtsell, Reverend James H. McGean, Cornelius M. O'Leary, Patrick Farrelly, Charles G. Herbermann, Marc F. Vallette, Thomas Addis Emmet, M.D., and Franklin Churchill. The aims of the society as set forth in its articles of incorporation were ambitious:

> The discovery, collection, and presentation of historical materials, relating to the introduction, establishment, and progress of the Catholic Church and Faith in the United States, to the progress of Christian art, and civilization therein, to Catholic American bibliography, and to evidences of Catholic Christianity furnished by American ethnology, linguistics and political developments, the discussion of subjects and the publication of essays, documents and rare books, relating to the above, and the maintenance of an historical library and museum of historical relics.[16]

Despite the comprehensive scope of its activities and the encouragement it received from the hierarchy, the society showed little signs of life from 1884 to 1886. In 1885 an effort was made

---

[14] "List of Historic Treasures in the Museum of the American Catholic Historical Society, May, 1933," *Records* XLIV (1933), 97–117. Cf. William J. Lallou, "The Archives of the American Catholic Historical Society (Philadelphia)," *Catholic Historical Review*, I (July, 1915), 193–195.

[15] T. J. Reardon, "The Society's Golden Jubilee," *Historical Records and Studies*, XXV (1935), 12.

[16] *Ibid.*, 8.

to amalgamate it with the Philadelphia society but no decision
was reached and the societies have existed separately since their
origin. Meantime, through the years 1885 and 1886, the society
published its proceedings.[17] Towards the close of the year 1886,
it was resolved to start the activity of the society by publishing
a quarterly magazine. With Shea as its editor, the first issue of
the official quarterly of the society appeared on January 1, 1887.
The new periodical was known as the *United States Catholic Historical Magazine* and was distinguished from the beginning by
the number and quality of the literary contributions made to it
from all parts of the United States.[18] From 1888 to 1892, when
Shea died, the *Magazine* appeared with fair regularity. In 1888,
a complete translation of Thormod Torfason's *History of Ancient Vinland* was made by Charles G. Herbermann and issued by
the society as a separate monograph; this was the forerunner to
the society's *Monograph Series.*[19] Without the services of Shea,
the publication of the quarterly was soon discovered to be an im-
possible task and from 1893 to 1897 the society was practically
inactive. During the interval, the only work it issued was a
*Columbus Memorial Volume* undertaken by Charles G. Herbermann and Marc F. Vallette. Efforts toward renewed activity
were made in 1898 when Archbishop Michael Corrigan took an
interest in the society. With the co-operation of the future Cardinal Farley, Charles G. Herbermann, Stephen and Patrick Farrelly,
Monsignori McGean and Brann, Father Campbell, S.J., Dr. Marc
Vallette and later John E. Cohalan, Thomas F. Meehan, Edward
J. McGuire, and Peter Condon, the society was given a new lease
on life. The vigor and ability of these few energetic historians
brought about in 1899 the publication of the *Historical Records
and Studies.* The papers published in this journal maintained from the beginning a high standard of historical scholar-

---

[17] Numbers 1–3.

[18] A catalogue of the contents of the *United States Catholic Historical
Magazine* is contained in the American Historical Association *Annual
Report,* II (1905), 134–136.

[19] Thormod Torfason, *The History of Ancient Vinland;* tr. from the
Latin of 1705 by Charles G. Herbermann (New York, 1888). Appended
to Volume II of the *United States Catholic Historical Magazine.*

ship. Many of the studies contributed are of a biographical nature, some of them containing important unpublished letters. One valuable diary, that of Father Juan A. Peña Bachiller, describing the advancement of the Aguayo expedition into Texas in 1722, is translated. This diary has a special value, since it stands ·in Catholic history at the beginning of the mission era in Texas. Besides the well-known study of Charles G. Herbermann on the Sulpician Society there are other important essays on the Capuchins and Jesuits. There are also five or six papers on Catholic schools and universities in the United States, including histories of the Universities of Notre Dame and Creighton, St. Mary's College, Fordham, and St. Mary's College, Wilmington, Delaware. The remaining studies appearing in the *Historical Records and Studies* are largely concerned with Catholic social problems, most of them being institutional and social in content. Thirty-three volumes of this periodical have been published up to 1943. No one volume index to the set has been issued, but indexes have been printed in Volumes XI, XIII, XIV, XV and XXX.[20]

Since 1902, the society has published intermittently *Monographs,* some of which are landmarks in Catholic American historiography. Although the majority of the monographs have been concerned with American Church history, a few of them are of value in the field of Americana. The monographs published to date are: *The Voyages of Christopher Columbus, As Told by the Discoverer; Unpublished Letters of Charles Carroll of Carrollton and of His Father, Charles Carroll of Doughoregan; Forty Years in the United States of America* (1839–1885) by Augustus J. Thébaud, S.J.; *Historical Sketch of St. Joseph's Provincial Seminary, Troy, New York,* by the Right Reverend Henry Gabriels, D.D.; *The Cosmographiae Introductio* of Martin Waldseemüller, in facsimile; *Three Quarters of a Century: 1807–*

---

[20] The index for the first ten Volumes is in Volume XI, 141–171; the index for Volumes XI–XII in Volume XIII, 190–196; the indexes for Volumes XIII and XIV in Volume XIV, 208–211, 212–213; the index for Volume XV in Volume XV, 153–156; and the index for Volumes XXV–XXIX in Volume XXX, 158–160. Volumes XVI–XXIV inclusive have not been indexed.

*1882*, two volumes, by Augustus J. Thébaud, S.J., *Diary of a Visit to the United States of America in the Year 1883* by Charles Lord Russell of Killowen; *St. Joseph's Seminary, Dunwoodie, New York, 1896–1921* by the Reverend Arthur J. Scanlan; *The Catholic Church in Virginia: 1815–1822* by Peter Guilday; *The Life of the Right Rev. John Baptist Mary David: 1761–1841* by Sister Columba Fox; *The Doctrina Breve* (Mexico, 1544) in facsimile; *Pioneer Catholic Journalism* by Paul J. Foik, C.S.C.; *Dominicans in Early Florida* by Victor F. O'Daniel, O.P.; *Pioneer German Catholics in the American Colonies: 1734–1784* by the Reverend Lambert Schrott; *The Leopoldine Foundation and the Church in the United States: 1829–1839* by Theodore Roemer, O.F.M.Cap.; *Gonzala de Tapia: 1561–1594, Founder of the First Permanent Jesuit Mission in North America* by W. Eugene Shiels, S.J.; *Old St. Peter's. The Mother Church of Catholic New York: 1785–1935* by Leo Raymond Ryan; *The Quebec Act: A Primary Cause of the American Revolution* by Charles H. Metzger, S.J.; *Catholic Immigrant Colonization Projects in the United States, 1815–1860* by Sister Mary Gilbert Kelly, O.P.

On February 22, 1892, Marc F. Vallette and George E. O'Hara organized the Long Island Catholic Historical Society, which changed its name when incorporated in 1894 to the Brooklyn Catholic Historical Society. The object of the society was to collect " all matters of an historical nature in relation to the Catholic Church, especially on Long Island." Among its more active members was the Rev. Dr. James R. Mitchell, whose *Golden Jubilee of Bishop Loughlin* (Brooklyn, 1891) gave him considerable local fame.[21] The organization was short-lived. It was responsible, however, for the Peter Turner Memorial in Brooklyn, and inaugurated the movement which led to the foundation of the Mitchell Memorial Scholarship at The Catholic University of America. One issue of a pamphlet called *Records* was printed in April, 1901, containing the following papers: " Early Catholic Explorers and Catholic Foundations of Long

---

[21] Cf. Peter Guilday, " Catholic Historical Societies in the United States," *Official Catholic Year Book for 1928* (New York, 1928), 642.

Island " by Marc F. Vallette; " Beginnings of the Roman Catholic Orphan Asylum Society " by Joseph W. Carroll; " Church of the Most Holy Trinity " from the manuscripts of John Gilmary Shea; and " Notes on Three Augustinian Missionaries in Brooklyn " by Thomas C. Middleton, O.S.A. Although plans for an official history of the diocese of Brooklyn were made in April, 1901, the society ceased to meet that year and was never revived.

The New England Catholic Historical Society was organized in Boston on June 13, 1900, under the auspices of the Very Rev. William Byrne, then vicar-general of the archdiocese. The objects of the society were:

> To promote Catholic historical research and a wider knowledge of the origins of the Catholic Church in New England; to make accessible documents and records relating to the same; to have made and preserved in each parish a careful record of ecclesiastical events; to promote especial study of distinguished churchmen and important events; to print from time to time approved monographs and lectures on the above-named topics; and to collect in one place historical materials.[22]

From 1901 to 1904 the society issued eight *Publications: First Report of the New England Catholic Historical Society; organized, June 13, 1900; The Early Irish Catholic Schools of Lowell, Massachusetts, 1835–1852* (Boston, 1901) by the Reverend Louis S. Walsh; *The Acadians of Madawaska, Maine* (Boston, 1902) by the Reverend Charles W. Collins; *Pilgrim, Puritan and Papist in Massachusetts* (Boston, 1902) by Helena Nordhoff Gargan; *Fr. Sebastian Rasle* (Boston, 1906) by the Reverend Arthur T. Connolly; *Memorial Volume of the One Hundredth Anniversary Celebration of the Dedication of the Church of the Holy Cross, Boston* (Boston, 1904) ; *An Appreciation of the Life and Labors of Rev. Francis Matignon, D.D.* (Boston, 1908) by the Reverend Arthur T. Connolly; and *Sketch of the Life and Missionary Labors of Rev. James Fitton* (Boston, 1908) by the Reverend L. P. McCarthy.

---

[22] *Ibid.*

As one of its main projects, the organization provided " that an effort should be made to have an historical record of every parish in New England secured and gathered together as a part of the preparation for a suitable celebration of the centenary of the archdiocese of Boston in 1908." [23]    The leading workers in the group were the authors of what is, up to the present time, one of the few worthy attempts at a provincial history of the Church in America: *The History of the Catholic Church in the New England States* (2 Vols., Boston, 1899).  Among the authors were the well known Right Reverend William Byrne, the Reverend James O'Donnell, the Reverend J. J. McCoy, the Most Reverend Austin Dowling, D.D. and the scholarly layman, William Leahy.  The society ceased to function after 1904.  Although the society was short-lived, it had accomplished much of the essential spadework that has facilitated the writing of a scholarly and critical history of the Church in New England by Fathers Robert H. Lord and John E. Sexton, the first volumes of which are now in press.

On April 25, 1905, Archbishop John Ireland, the bishops of the ecclesiastical province of St. Paul, the Abbot of St. John's Abbey, Collegeville, Minnesota, and a large number of priests from St. Paul and Minneapolis, met at the St. Paul Seminary and organized the St. Paul Catholic Historical Society. Archbishop Ireland, who had taken an active part in the formation of the United States Catholic Historical Society, thought the time opportune for the formation of a society to study the Catholic history of the Northwest.  The object of the new society, therefore, was to collect and preserve materials of all kinds relating to the Catholic history, not only of St. Paul but of the Northwest.  In December, 1912, at a special meeting of the officers for the purpose of reorganizing and incorporating the society, its name was changed to the Catholic Historical Society of St. Paul.[24]  In 1907, the society began the publication of its researches in its official periodical *Acta et Dicta*.  Although origi-

---

[23] *Ibid.*

[24] " The St. Paul Catholic Historical Society," *Acta et Dicta,* I (July, 1907), 7.

nally intended as a semi-annual volume, *Acta et Dicta* appeared irregularly, two issues to the volume, until 1918. After 1918, the society was inactive until 1933 when it was completely reorganized. In 1934, it re-issued its *Acta et Dicta.*

This periodical had from the beginning a scholarly character and has taken its place beside the leading Catholic historical reviews. In the seven volumes published up to the year 1935, the research student of the old Northwest will find much material of inestimable value. Among the letters and allied documents it has printed are the translated letters of Bishop Joseph Cretin, the correspondence of Bishop Mathias Loras, then a missionary priest, the *Memorialis Tabella* or diary of Cretin and a missionary journal kept by Bishop Grace. Excellent studies on the various aspects of missionary activity in the Northwest occupy many pages of the periodical; they include Sister M. Aquinas Norton's "Missionary Activity in the Northwest under the French Regime, 1640–1740;" Thomas O'Gorman's study of the early French exploration within the borders of South Dakota; Sister Ignatius Loyola Cox's "The Mission at St. Anthony Falls, or East Minneapolis;" Chrysostom Verwyst's account of the Fond du Lac Indian Mission; and Edwin V. O'Hara's "Father De Smet in the Ecclesiastical Province of St. Paul." There is a good account of the Sisters of St. Joseph in Minnesota as well as several papers on Catholic colonization projects in the same area. There is also a comprehensive and scholarly paper by A. J. Rezek on the Leopoldine Society. Besides the "Life of Rt. Rev. Joseph Cretin" by Archbishop John Ireland, which runs through several volumes of the journal, there are a number of other biographical studies of important figures in the spread of Catholicism in the Northwest.[25] There are numerous studies on the parochial and institutional development of the Church in St. Paul, Minnesota. Not least among the more valuable studies are the essays on the growth of the Church in various sections of

---

[25] The subjects of these biographies include: Father Louis Hennepin, Father Lawrence Lautiskar, Captain William B. McGrorty, Father Pierz, Father Francis Pirec, Father Samuel Charles Mazzuchelli, O.P., and Father Lacombe.

the Northwest: " The Beginning of Catholicism in North Dakota " by Bishop John Shanley; " Catholicity in North Dakota "
by Joseph B. McDonald; " The Catholic Church in Wright
County, Minnesota " by Mathias Savs; " The Catholic Church in
Goodhue County, Minnesota " by J. H. Gaughan; " The History
of the Diocese of St. Paul " by Francis J. Schaefer; " The Beginnings and Growth of the Catholic Church in the State of Mon-
tana " by Cyril Pauwelyn; and " Notes on the History of the
Diocese of Duluth " by Patrick J. Lydon.

The Maine Catholic Historical Society was tentatively started
by Bishop Louis Walsh in 1908 on the occasion of the centennial
celebration of St. Patrick's Church at Damariscotta. A permanent organization was not effected, however, until April 25,
1911.[26] The objects of the society were: (1) The research and
publication of whatever is important in person, fact or document
regarding the original growth of the Catholic Church in the present State of Maine; (2) to assist similar societies in the State
and Country, by affiliation and cooperation, to spread the life and
truth and light of the Catholic Church.[27] The purpose of the
society's publication, *The Maine Catholic Historical Magazine*,
which appeared in July, 1913, was to give " an accurate and complete record of all past and present events of the Diocese of Portland, all official reports of institutions, the official documents and
a chronology of all important events in the diocese." [28] The
*Magazine* was actually the official bulletin of the diocese of Portland. As such, it was, from a critical standpoint, far below all
the Catholic historical periodicals that had been published up to
that time. In the eight volumes that appeared between 1913 and
October, 1919, when it ceased publication, there were few articles
of a critical or scholarly nature. Besides a host of *memorabilia*
that will always prove useful to the historian of the Catholic
Church in this country, the most valuable contributions made in
its pages are a lengthy study on the Catholic Church in Maine
which runs through all eight volumes, and accounts of the celebra-

---

[26] " Catholic Historical Society Comment," *Records*, XXIV (1913), 280.
[27] *Ibid.*
[28] *Ibid.*

tions held in honor of the tercentenary of the Catholic Church in Maine.

In 1916, the officers of the society were able to announce that

> the threads of the Catholic history of Maine from 1604 have been gathered up and the chief historic events have been carefully recorded, while the chronology of the present and all important Church events have been printed.  Historical material of great importance has been collected from Maine, Quebec, Baltimore, Boston and a few other places, and the story of the past three hundred years will be placed before our people until every important person, place or event in the Catholic history of Maine will have been made known to our people.[29]

The organization on February 7, 1917, of the Catholic Historical Society of St. Louis was, as it has been aptly described by one of its founders, " the result of a century's endeavor."   As far back as the time of Bishop Joseph Rosati, the first bishop of the see, the clergy and laity of St. Louis had recognized the importance of the historic past of their church and had shown a desire to collect the *monumenta historica* of old " Louisiana."  The archdiocesan archives are filled with the materials gathered from 1818 to 1848 under Bishop Rosati's inspiration.[30]   The initial attempt to organize a society for this purpose came as early as 1878, when the Ecclesiastico-Historical Society of St. Louis was begun by some of the clergy.[31]   Among the men founding the society were: the Very Rev. Henry Van der Sanden and Fathers James Henry, W. H. Brantner, James J. McCabe, C. Ziegler and H. Leygraff.   The success of the Ecclesiastico-Historical Society did not fulfill the expectations of its founders, except that its president, Monsignor Henry Van der Sanden, added to the archives many new treasures in the form of transcripts from Roman documents.   Impressed with the importance of the Rosati papers,

---

[29] Guilday, " Catholic Historical Societies," *loc. cit.,* 643.

[30] John Rothensteiner, " The Catholic Historical Society of St. Louis, the Result of a Century's Endeavor," *St. Louis Catholic Historical Review,* I (1918), 11.

[31] *Ibid.,* 12.

he sought to increase the collection by adding most of the official documents issued during the long period of his chancellorship. In 1882, he went to Rome and copied many letters and other documents bearing on the early history of the diocese of St. Louis.[32]  In this important work Van der Sanden had the advice and help of John Gilmary Shea with whom he was in correspondence.  Despite efforts to keep the society active on the part of such scholars and editors as the Rev. David Phelan of *Western Watchman*, F. P. Kenkel of *Amerika,* and *Central Blatt and Social Justice,* Paul Chew of *Church Progress* and Rev. F. G. Holweck of the *St. Louis Pastoral-Blatt* the original enthusiasm died out.  A few years later, the Catholic Union of Missouri founded an historical commission for the purpose of gathering, collating and preserving the materials for a history of the German Catholics in the State.  Apart from a *History of the Church in St. Louis,* written by a member of the Commission, little was accomplished, but the project was never lost to sight and many valuable historical essays on the subject have been published in the *Central Blatt and Social Justice* of the Catholic Central Verein of North America.[33]  Finally, in 1917, Archbishop Glennon invited a number of priests to meet for the purpose of forming the Catholic Historical Society of St. Louis.  The moment was well chosen since the centennial of the Church in St. Louis was to be observed the following year.  The object of the society was

> to collect and preserve materials of all kinds, such as books, pamphlets, papers, manuscripts, maps, documents, pictures and other objects of historic interest relating to the Catholic history of the Diocese of St. Louis and of whatever territories and places were at any time associated with St. Louis in the same ecclesiastical division; to institute, carry on, and foster historical research

[32] F. G. Holweck, "The Historical Archives of the Archdiocese of St. Louis," *St. Louis Catholic Historical Review,* I (1918), 24–39.

[33] This organization has carried an invaluable historical section in its official publication *Central Blatt and Social Justice* (now *Social Justice Review*).  The Central Verein also has an historical library where there is housed a remarkable collection of books, brochures, newspapers, magazines and manuscripts.

on subjects pertaining to the field of inquiry above described,[34] and disseminate such information.

In October, 1918, the society issued the first number of its official periodical *The St. Louis Catholic Historical Review* with Charles L. Souvay, C.M., as its editor-in-chief, assisted by a group of noted Catholic scholars, among whom were: the Reverend F. G. Holweck, Gilbert J. Garraghan, S.J., the Reverend John Rothensteiner and Edward Brown. The *Review* was an immediate success and gave evidence of fresh strength in the growing influence of Catholic historical studies in the United States; it immediately took precedence for scholarship and historical value among all similar reviews in this country. The documents published in each number, the lists of manuscript sources, and the catalogues of historical sources and works on the Church in old " Louisiana " were superbly done. Nothing comparable to the contents of the *Review* had appeared before in Catholic American literature.

The *Review* continued to be issued quarterly until October, 1923, when the society ceased to function. In the five volumes issued between 1918 and 1923, a large number of letters and allied documents were published for the first time. Among these were the diary of Bishop Rosati covering the period August, 1822 to December, 1826; the diary of the journey of the Sisters of St. Joseph to Tucson, Arizona; a number of documents in regard to the participation of the priest, Angelo Inglesi, in the " Hogan war between the Bishop of Philadelphia and the trustees of St. Mary's Church; " the correspondence of Bishop Du Bourg with the Sacred Congregation de Propaganda Fide, 1819–1829; letters of Father Beauprez, 1831–1835, Father Stephen Badin, 1829, Father Joseph Prost, 1836, Bishop Edward Fenwick, 1832 and of Archbishop James Whitfield to Bishop Rosati, 1828–1834. There is also a calendar of documents (1814–1868) from the archives of Propaganda Fide, copies of which had been secured by the society. F. G. Holweck's excellent study " The Historical Archives of the Archdiocese of St. Louis " gives a

---

[34] Rothensteiner, *loc. cit.*, 8.

history of its development and lists in detail all the important matters among the documents, petitions, Mexicana, and letters. The *Review* abounds in critical studies on the missions in Missouri, Illinois, Iowa, Arkansas and Louisiana done by some of the leading Catholic historical scholars. The subjects of the biographical studies include Father Edmond Saulnier, Abbé Joseph Anthony Lutz, Father Henri Pratte, Father James Maxwell, Father Charles Nerinckx, Rev. John Francis Regis Loisel, Alexander Bellesime, and Alexander McNair. In 1918, shortly after its foundation, the society maintained for a time an archivist in Rome, copying in the Roman archives documents bearing on the early history of the St. Louis Archdiocese. The archives of the society have been kept in the archdiocesan chancery.

The Illinois Catholic Historical Society was founded in 1918 in preparation for the centenary of the admission of the State into the Union and the diamond jubilee of the diocese of Chicago (1919). The need for collecting and putting into some permanent form the scattered record of the Church in Illinois had been long recognized. When the Illinois Centenary Commission announced its intention of publishing a comprehensive history of Illinois to celebrate the one hundredth anniversary of the admission of the State into the Union, Father Frederick Seidenberg, S.J., at that time head of the department of sociology at Loyola University, Chicago, and a member of the Commission, realized the necessity of organizing a society to make better known the work of the Catholics in Illinois. Accordingly, he called together all those interested in the project and on February 28, 1918, with the approval of Archbishop Mundelein, this group launched the Illinois Catholic Historical Society. Among the organizers of the society were many well known figures in historical circles: William J. Onahan, its first president, Father Seidenburg, James A. Graham, Margaret Madden, Rt. Rev. Daniel J. Riordan, Edward Brown, Joseph J. Thompson, the first editor of the society's publication, Rev. Frederick Beuckman, Rev. J. B. Culemans, Rev. Francis J. Epstein and William Stetson Merrill. The primary purpose of the society was to survey and study the

Catholic history of Illinois, to collect historical works, documents, records, relics and mementos of the Church in that State, and to disseminate a knowledge of Catholic history by means of lectures and publications.[35]   One of the first activities provided for by the society was the publication of a quarterly magazine known as the *Illinois Catholic Historical Review,* eleven volumes of which appeared under this title.   In July, 1929, the *Review* changed its name to *Mid-America.*   The new policy adopted by the journal was, as its name indicates, more comprehensive in scope, concerning itself with the record of Catholic life and history in the entire Mississippi Valley.

The *Illinois Catholic Historical Review* and its successor *Mid-America* have now reached their twenty-fifth volume and they rank among the important historical journals in the country.   During the first twenty-four years of its existence the staff of the *Review* consisted of such competent historical scholars as Gilbert J. Garraghan, S.J., Paul J. Foik, C.S.C., Francis Borgia Steck, O.F.M., Samuel K. Wilson, S.J., Sister Mary Celeste Leger, R.S.M., Peter Leo Johnson, W. Eugene Shiels, S.J., Raphael Hamilton, S.J., Raymond Corrigan, S.J., Jean Delanglez, S.J., Paul Kiniery, Francis V. Corrigan and J. Manuel Espinosa.   Each number of the quarterly, without exception, has been replete with articles of importance to the Catholic history of the Middle West, the old French lands and the States established in that vast territory.   The journal abounds in highly valued studies on the early missions and the religious communities which helped to make them the success they were, particularly those of the Jesuits, Franciscans, Vincentians, Sulpicians, the Society of Mary and the Christian Brothers.   Of the religious communities of women, the Sisters of St. Francis, Sisters of Charity of St. Augustine, the Ursuline Sisters, the Sisters of Mercy and the Visitandine nuns are given the most attention.   There are also excellent essays on the various racial stocks in the Middle West, the better studies being on the Germans, Irish and Slovaks.   A considerable portion of the history of Catholic education and the

---

[35] " The Illinois Catholic Historical Society," *Illinois Catholic Historical Review,* I (July, 1918), 137.

Indian problem in this area has likewise been done. The *Review* has published many documents of paramount importance such as the *Exposition* of Don Juan Antonio de Trasvina Retis and the narratives of a missionary journey to Santa Fé made by the Sisters of Loretto. There are also excellent translations of Bishop Blanchet's journal, Espinosa's diary relating to his entry into Texas in 1716; sections from the diary and gazette of Father Pierre Potico, S.J., and a reprinting of Nicholas Point's journal.

Among the important correspondence it prints for the first time are: the letters of Bishop Pierre Jean Loras, 1833–1849; the letters of John Grassi, S.J. to Simon Bruté de Remur, 1812–1832; three letters of Father Jeremiah F. Trecy containing much data on the pioneer Catholic history of Nebraska from 1859 to 1860; the letters of Bishop William Quarter to Joseph Picquet between 1844 and 1847; two letters of Bishop Van de Velde, S.J., to the Prince Bishop of Vienna, 1850–1851, taken from the *Berichte;* excerpts from the correspondence of Bishop John Baptist Miège, S.J., to his brother in France, edited and annotated; Bishop England's correspondence with Bishop Rosati from 1826–1838; sixteen letters of Bishop Benedict Joseph Fenwick to Bishop Rosati covering the years 1830–1840; letters written to the Very Reverend John Timon, C.M., from Kaskaskia and other missions in the Illinois country, 1835–1843; and correspondence on Indian removal in Indiana, 1835–1838. The outstanding biographical studies are on Father Pierre Gibault, Father Gabriel de la Ribourde, Father Pierre De Smet, Right Reverend Julian Benoit, Archbishop John Lancaster Spalding, William J. Onahan, Bishop Peter James Muldoon, Archbishop Peter Richard Kenrick, Bishop Bruté, Venerable Antonio Margil de Jesus, Bishop Duggan, Oliver Pollock, William Lamprecht, Colonel Richard O'Sullivan Burke, William A. Amberg, John P. Hopkins, Louis Jolliet, Colonel Daniel E. McCarthy, Colonel John Montgomery, Father Sebastien Louis Meurin, Father De La Valinière, John George Alleman, O.P., Charles Felix Van Quickenborne, S.J., Father Saint Cyr, Reverend William de la Porte, Reverend Dennis Ryan, Claude Jean Allouez, S.J., Bishop Van de Velde and Reverend George Henry Ostlangenberg. Studies of special merit on the

Church in Mid-America are those of Joseph J. Thompson, " Illinois, the Cradle of Christianity and Civilization in Mid-America; " John Rothensteiner, " Historical Antecedents of the Diocese of St. Louis; " Sister Ursula Thomas, " The Catholic Church on the Oklahoma Frontier; " Gilbert J. Garraghan, " Old Vincennes, a Chapter in the Ecclesiastical History of the West; " and Charles F. Griffith, " Catholic Beginnings in Southeastern Iowa." Other adequate studies are: Francis John Connors, " Samuel Finley Breese Morse and the Anti-Catholic Movements in the United States (1791–1872) ; " Joseph J. Thompson, " The Knights of Columbus in the War and After; " Anthony Matre, " The American Federation of Catholic Societies; " and Frank L. Reynolds, " The Ancient Order of Hibernians."

The nine Catholic historical societies which had been founded in the twenty-five years that had passed since the Third Plenary Council (1884–1919) had confined themselves to research and study in the field of American Church history. On December 30, 1919, the American Catholic Historical Association was established at Cleveland by Peter Guilday and a group of some sixty Catholic scholars and writers of history. Unlike all the societies that had preceded it, the American Catholic Historical Association had been formed to direct its research into the wider field of general Catholic history.[36] The officers of the Association elected at the Cleveland meeting included many of the foremost Catholic historical scholars in the country: President, Lawrence F. Flick, Vice-Presidents, Richard H. Tierney, S.J., and Victor O'Daniel, O.P., Secretary, Carlton J. H. Hayes; Archivist, Peter Guilday. The Executive Council included, with the above named officers, Reverend Gilbert P. Jennings, Right Reverend Monsignor Joseph F. Mooney, Dr. Charles Souvay, C.M., Reverend William Busch and Zephyrim Engelhardt, O.F.M. The official headquarters of the Association were permanently fixed at The Catholic University of America in Washington. Since 1919, the Association has held twenty-four

---

[36] The fullest account of the organization of the Association is Peter Guilday, " The American Catholic Historical Association," *Catholic Mind,* XVIII (June, 1920), 227–236.

annual meetings in all sections of the country for the purpose of mutual help and encouragement. The number and variety of the papers read at its annual sessions show how successfully the Association has followed the lines it laid down at its foundation. These essays have considered almost every phase of the historical past of the Church including the problems of Church and State, civil and ecclesiastical law, concordats, education, conversions, the reunion of Christendom, Catholic charities, nationalism, ecclesiastical historiography, and the Catholic philosophy of history.

In addition to the annual meetings, the Association has sponsored three publications: (1) the *Papers* of the Association, containing the contributions to a subject which occasionally forms the single topic of an annual meeting; (2) the *Documents* of the Association, which are collections of primary sources bearing upon some phase of Catholic Church history; and (3) *The Catholic Historical Review*, the official organ of the Association. Three volumes of its *Papers* have been published to date: I, *Church Historians* (New York, 1926), being the papers read at the Ann Arbor meeting in 1925; II, the *Catholic Church in Contemporary Europe: 1919–1931* (New York, 1932), comprising the papers read at the Minneapolis meeting in 1931; and III, *The Catholic Philosophy of History* (New York, 1934), being the papers read at the Pittsburgh meeting in 1933. Of its *Documents,* one volume has been published: Dr. Leo F. Stock's *United States Ministers to the Papal States: Instructions and Dispatches, 1848–1868* (Washington, D. C., 1933); Volume II, *United States Consuls to the Papal States, Instructions and Dispatches,* is in an advanced stage of preparation. The *Catholic Historical Review* became the official organ of the Association in 1922. The *Review* had been founded in 1915 at The Catholic University of America under the inspiration of Bishop Thomas J. Shahan and Professor Guilday. It was founded for the purpose of keeping Catholic scholars *au courant* of all that was being done by their co-workers in the same and allied fields. From the beginning the periodical was national in scope and character and aimed primarily at dealing with the history of the Catholic Church in the United States. Besides Bishop Shahan and Dr. Guilday, the

*Review* in its early years was staffed with many well-known priests and scholars such as Victor F. O'Daniel, O.P., Patrick J. Healy, William Turner, Paschal Robinson, O.F.M., and Nicholas A. Weber, S.M.

Until 1921 the *Catholic Historical Review,* under the careful and enthusiastic direction of Guilday, published a remarkable series of articles, miscellanies, documents, book reviews, notes and comments, and bibliographies in the field of American Church history. A glance at the documents published in the first six volumes of the *Review* will show how valuable these volumes are for the student of Catholic Church history. They include: an early pastoral letter (1827) by Bishop Edward Fenwick, O.P.; documents of King Charles III of Spain, making provisions for building St. Peter's Church in Barclay Street, New York; papers from the collection of Archbishop Purcell, 1857–1862; Bishop Flaget's report of the diocese of Bardstown to Pius VII (April 10, 1815); the diocese of Baltimore in 1818—Archbishop Maréchal's account to Propaganda, October 16, 1818; documents relating to the election of Bishop Concanen to New York; documents from Propaganda archives appointing Dom Didier as prefect-apostolic of a projected French colony; documents on the first episcopal visitation in the United States (1606); the Jesuit Missions in 1773; Brassac's correspondence with the American bishops; Archbishop John Hughes, Lincoln's envoy to France (1861); the Medieval American Church; a bishop for the Indians in 1790; selected letters from the Roux correspondence; an account of the voyage of the *Princesa* and *Favorita* (1799); Episcopology of Puerto Rico; the Decho Fages manuscripts on California, Bishop Purcell's journal, (1833–1836); Guilday's guide to the materials for American Church history in the Westminster archdiocesan archives (1675–1798); some letters of Fathers Badin and Nerinckx to Bishop Carroll; appointment of Father John Carroll as Prefect-Apostolic (1783–1785); the earliest printed history of the United States; and *Ragguaglio dello Stato della Religione Cattolica nelle Colonie inglesi d'America.*

With the April issue of 1921, the *Review* abandoned the national field for the broader sphere of general Catholic history. The character of the *Review* changed considerably since it contained fewer studies on the Church in America. Since 1922, as the official publication of the Association, it has printed many of the papers read at the annual meetings. The journal is now in its twenty-ninth volume. A general index of the *Review* for the years 1915–1934 has been compiled by the Reverend Harold J. Bolton.

Another organization, the Texas Knights of Columbus Commission, was formed on May 15–16, 1923, at the twentieth annual convention of the Texas State Council of the Knights of Columbus, Austin, Texas. Working in harmony with the University of Texas and the State Historical Association, the commission spent several years copying and collecting data of all kinds to be found in that rich field of early Catholic history. The work accomplished during the years is chronicled in the printed *Minutes* of each annual meeting. The purpose for which the commission was founded was to prepare a centennial history of the Church in Texas (1836–1936) in honor of the approaching anniversary of Texas independence. As an auxiliary to the commission, the Texas Catholic Historical Society was formed in 1926 under Paul J. Foik, C.S.C., chairman of the commission and president of the society. The society has its headquarters at St. Edward's University, Austin, Texas. Incorporated in 1936, it meets semi-annually and publishes a quarterly: *Preliminary Studies of the Texas Catholic Historical Society,* containing essays of value to the historical student, many of them reprints from the various leading historical journals in the country. Seven volumes of the commission's monumental history of the Church in Texas have been published under the title: *Our Catholic Heritage in Texas* (Austin, 1936–     ).

The Catholic Historical Society of Indiana was begun on October 27, 1926, at Indianapolis to prepare a complete history of the Catholic Church in Indiana for the centennial of the diocese of Vincennes-Indianapolis in 1934. The aims of the society as given by Gilbert J. Garraghan, S.J., in his inaugural address were threefold: To collect the materials for Indiana Catholic history; to house them securely and preserve them permanently in a place where they may be at the service of students and investigators; and finally, to build eventually on the materials so assembled an adequate written record of the Church's glorious past in Indiana and secure for this record the widest possible publicity.[37]  Since its foundation, however, the society has not been active having published only one small *Bulletin* to date.

In March, 1928, the Iowa Catholic Historical Society was founded at Dubuque under the presidency of Archbishop James J. Keane and with the assistance of members of the faculty of Columbia (now Loras) College.  The purpose of the society was " to collect and preserve material facts and data of an historical nature, books, pamphlets, maps, portraits, paintings, relics, manu-scripts, letters, documents and any and all articles and materials which may establish or illustrate the Catholic history of Iowa or adjoining states; and of publishing such historical matter as the society may authorize." [38]  The college library was designated as the official depository of the society.  The first publication to ap-pear under the auspices of the society was the *Collections,* the first number of which was written by the Reverend M. M. Hoff-mann and titled: *The Catholic Sponsors of Iowa* (n.p., n.d.), an account of the military and political careers of General George W. Jones and General Augustus C. Dodge, who were the first to represent the State of Iowa in the United States Senate.  In Jan-uary, 1930, the first issue of the official organ of the society, the *Iowa Catholic Historical Review,* made its appearance.  In the nine volumes of the *Review* that have been issued to date there are many excellent papers on the history of the Church in Iowa. Some titles are: " Sources in Early Iowa Catholic History; " " An Epic of Early Iowa: Father Trecy's Colonization Scheme; " " Beginnings of Catholicity in Des Moines; " " Catholic Writers of Iowa ; " " Canon Vivaldi's Missionary Activities ; " " Bohemian (Czech) Catholics in Iowa; " " History of the Catholic Press in

---

[37] Gilbert J. Garraghan, " The Purpose of a Catholic Historical So-ciety," *Illinois Catholic Historical Review,* X (July, 1927), 15–25.

[38] " The Constitution," *Iowa Catholic Historical Review,* I (1930), 29.

Iowa;" "Europe's Pennies and Iowa's Missions;" "Loras in Alabama;" "The Foundation of the Catholic Church in Poca- hontas County;" "Father F. J. Bonduel, Missioner;" "The Old- est College in Iowa (Loras);" "Beginnings of the Catholic Church in Northwest Iowa, with Special Reference to Emmets- burg and Palo Alto County;" "Clement Smyth, Second Bishop of Iowa;" and "The Church in Early Iowa City—a New Light on the First Franciscan Father in Iowa and on Bishop Clement Smyth, 1864–1865."

Father Hoffman has been the editor of the *Review* from the beginning and has contributed some valuable essays, many of which were preliminary to his longer studies on *Antique Dubuque, 1673–1833* (Dubuque, Iowa, 1930), *The Church Foun- ders of the Northwest; Loras and Cretin and Other Captains of Christ* (Dubuque, Iowa, 1938), the *Centennial History of the Archdiocese of Dubuque* (Dubuque, Iowa, 1938), a compilation of which he is editor, and *The Story of Loras College, 1839– 1939* (Dubuque, Iowa, 1939). The society has published a sec- ond volume in its *Collections:* C. F. Griffith, *Saint Peter's Parish, Keokuk, Iowa, 1832–1929* (Keokuk, Iowa, 1929).

Since the Iowa foundation only one new Catholic historical society of note has been founded. The Kansas Catholic Histori- cal Society was organized in 1930 at St. Benedict's College, Atchison, Kansas. It has been collecting books, pamphlets, manu- scripts and other materials relating to the Catholic history of the State and today has one of the best collections of its kind. For a number of years the society was inactive but was revived in 1939, though it has not yet published anything of importance in the field. The first fruits of this research will be found in Peter Beckman's *History of the Catholic Church in Kansas* (Washing- ton, D. C., 1944).

The influence that these Catholic historical societies have had on the advancement of American Catholic historiography is not too easily measured. They did bring together for personal as- sociation and for important academic discussion the leading Catholic and many non-Catholic scholars, thereby putting the younger writers in touch with the older historians. In almost every instance they have provided, through their various publications, channels of expression for historical scholars and thus have made easier the path of the future historian. Through their journals, they have likewise set standards of achievement which have done much to raise the status of the historian of the Catholic Church in this country to an equality with that of investigators in secular history and other fields of research. The securing and publication of documents from home and abroad has attracted the interest of national and state historical societies and many noted scholars in American history. Co-operation has made possible an accuracy in detail and variety of treatment unattainable in individual production and non-existent in the field of American Catholic history before 1884. Finally, collaboration, which the societies foster, has led to the execution of larger projects in the field of American Catholic history.

# CHAPTER IV

## Historiography of the American Catholic Church: 1884–1915

THE intellectual awakening in the field of Catholic historical scholarship prompted by the Letter of Pope Leo XIII and the pioneer work of the father of American Catholic Church history, John Gilmary Shea, resulted in one of the more productive periods in American Catholic historiography.

The development of research turned the Catholic scholar to the documentary evidence upon which to build his history. As critical scholars gradually verified the historical records of the Church, they could be safely used with greater confidence. From the time of Shea down to 1915, a succession of talented men collected, transcribed and edited all they could find of records pertaining to the Catholic Church in America. Campbell, Spalding, Bayley, Rosati, Hassard, Maes, Webb, O'Connell, Lambing, Alerding, Moosmueller and Sarah Brownson are only a few of those who were active in American Catholic historiography before the turn of the twentieth century. Not one of those who wrote during the thirty year period under consideration (1884–1915) had the advantages of formal training in the study of American Church history; but, commencing as an avocation, it gradually grew to be an absorbing passion in their lives. The direct result was a wealth of writings on various aspects of the history of the Church in America. This literature can be classified conveniently under six broad headings: (1) provincial histories; (2) diocesan histories; (3) parochial histories; (4) institutional histories; (5) ecclesiastical biographies and (6) monographs of a miscellaneous nature.

Writing in the same period as Shea, but not coming under his direct influence, were several notable authors. The first, and perhaps the one who did most to promote an interest in Catholic history, was Colonel Bernard U. Campbell (1795–1855). Campbell was one of the earliest serious workers in American Catholic history and will be remembered for his life-long efforts to collect and preserve materials for the history of the Church in the United States. He never wrote a book, but he did write for the *United States Catholic Magazine* a life of Archbishop John Carroll and other pertinent studies which appeared in the leading periodicals of the day. Of especial value is a paper he read before the Maryland Historical Society in 1846 entitled "Early Missions Among the Indians in Maryland."[1] Although the field has been worked to better advantage since his time by Shea, Thomas Hughes and others, this study is representative of the state of historical scholarship among American Catholics at the time. Shea describes Campbell as "patient, accurate, sound in judgment, clear and interesting in his statement of facts" and admits that his publications have been "a great storehouse for later writers." Shea acknowledged that Campbell had been a great aid to him "by his printed work, and by many of his transcripts."[2]

Another outstanding pioneer in this period of American Catholic historiography was Bishop Joseph Rosati (1789–1843).[3] A native Italian, Rosati entered the Congregation of the Mission in Rome in 1807. In the following year he began his theological studies under Father Andrew James Felix Bartholomew De-Andreis. After his ordination in 1811, he spent five years in home mission work and then he joined DeAndreis on the Louisiana mission. Rosati had been an intimate friend of DeAndreis, and upon the latter's death, succeeded him as superior of the Congregation of the Mission in America. In 1824, Rosati was consecrated bishop and administered the dioceses of New Orleans and St. Louis until 1830. Despite the burden of mission duties in

---

[1] Reprinted in *Maryland Historical Magazine,* I (1906), 293–316.

[2] John Gilmary Shea, *A History of the Catholic Church in the United States* (New York, 1892), IV, 376 and footnote 3, 376–377.

[3] Charles L. Souvay, "Joseph Rosati," *Dictionary of American Biography,* XVI, 155–156. Cf. John Frederick Easterly, *The Life of Rt. Rev. Joseph Rosati, C.M., First Bishop of St. Louis: 1789–1843* (Washington, D. C., 1942).

Louisiana and the surrounding territory, Rosati found time to gather the materials for his *Life of the Very Rev. Felix De-Andreis, C.M.* In 1840, with his manuscript in Italian, he went to Rome with the intention of having the work first published in Italy. The Italian life, however, was never published because of the death in 1843 of Rev. J. B. Samaria, an Oratorian priest of Turin, who had agreed to collect further information about the early life of Father DeAndreis and to prepare the work for the printer. Francis Burlando, C.M., translated the manuscript into English and had it published in Baltimore in 1861.[4] Rosati's narrative was clear and accurate enough to make his volume a source book for Catholic history in and around Louisiana.

The desire to preserve the details of early Catholic life in this country was the main reason that Martin John Spalding (1810–1872) became one of the first historians of Kentucky. A native of this region, he attended in his early years a typical log-cabin school and later graduated from St. Mary's College, near Lebanon, in 1826. He then entered the seminary at Bardstown, where he came into contact with such Catholic pioneers as Bishop Benedict J. Flaget and his coadjutor, John B. M. David, and Francis Patrick Kenrick. In 1830, he was sent to the Urban College, Rome, where he won the friendship of John England, the future Cardinals Wiseman and Cullen, and Monsignor Capellari, the future Pope Gregory XVI. Ordained in 1834, he returned to Bardstown where he became pastor of the Cathedral and instructor in the seminary. Spalding began his literary career early, both as editor and contributor to such literary magazines as the *Catholic Advocate, Louisville Guardian, Religious Cabinet, The United States Catholic Magazine,* and the *Metropolitan.* In 1844, after he had won renown throughout the United States and Canada as a lecturer, he was called to Louisville by Bishop Flaget to be vicar-general. In 1848, he was consecrated bishop to serve as coadjutor with the right of succession, but did not formally succeed until February 11, 1850. During his administration he showed great zeal in building up the diocese and in

---

[4] Cf. Archbishop John J. Kain's introduction to the new and revised edition (St. Louis, 1900), v–xiii.

quelling the Know-nothing agitation stirred up by the *Louisville Daily Journal*. In 1844, he published the first of his historical writings: *Sketches of the Early Catholic Missions of Kentucky from Their Commencement in 1787 to the Jubilee of 1826–27* (Louisville, 1844).[5]

The purpose of this historical study was "to collect together, and to record, in a series of sketches, such facts as might prove interesting to the general reader, and serve as materials for the future Church historian of the United States, and especially of the West, to which Kentucky has been, in a religious, if not in a political, point of view, the great pioneer and *alma mater*."[6] Spalding accomplished his purpose by giving to future historians an authoritative source book for the early Catholic missions in Kentucky. He gathered his materials from every source within his reach. He not only collected accurate accounts from all the pioneers still living in his own time, but he relied to a great extent upon written and printed documents when these were available. He searched the *Annales* of the Propagation of the Faith and many of the religious journals published in America and Europe. His chief source seems to have been the accurate and well-written account of the early missions of Kentucky drawn up by Father Stephen Theodore Badin and printed in Paris in 1822.[7] He also had the personal aid of Badin who filled in many of the *lacunae* in the materials furnished by the printed documents. Because Spalding was unable to procure sources for the later portion of the history, this section of the volume is less detailed. Although he wrote many studies of an apologetic and historical nature between 1844 and 1870, Spalding's most important contribution to American Catholic historiography was made in his *Sketches of the Life, Times, and Character of the Rev. Benedict Joseph*

---

[5] Richard J. Purcell, "Martin John Spalding," *Dictionary of American Biography*, XVII, 424–426. Cf. J. L. Spalding, *The Life of the Most Rev. M. J. Spalding, D.D., Archbishop of Baltimore* (New York, 1873).

[6] Spalding, *Sketches*, v.

[7] Father Badin's work on the missions is titled: *Origine et Progrès de la Mission du Kentucky (États-Unis d'Amérique)* Paris, 1821. It is translated in the *United States Catholic Miscellany* (Dec., 1824), and in the *Catholic World* (Sept., 1875), 825–835.

*Flaget, First Bishop of Louisville* (Louisville, 1852). Again, Spalding endeavored to preserve the records for future historians, this time by writing the life of one who was identified with the early history of the Catholic Church in the West and South for a period of over fifty years. For his sources, he used the personal reminiscences of the prelate as recorded by his private secretary, Father Peter J. Lavialle; Flaget's own manuscript journal, begun in 1812 and continued until 1834, with an additional separate account of his visit to Rome in 1836; his correspondence which was extensive as well as voluminous; the French *Life* of Flaget, written by Abbé Desgeorges, his traveling companion on his last visit to Europe; and documents from the diocesan archives of Baltimore, St. Louis, Cincinnati, New Orleans and Pittsburgh. With these studies, Spalding established himself as one of the ablest of the earlier group of American Catholic writers who wrote primarily to preserve the data on the early history of the Church. He was a diligent and thorough worker with keen historical judgment, and his two contributions to Catholic historiography have been rich sources for later historians.

James Roosevelt Bayley (1814–1877) became a Catholic in 1842. After completing his studies for the priesthood, Bayley was ordained in 1844 and nine years later, 1853, was appointed bishop of Newark and in 1872 became archbishop of Baltimore. Not a profound scholar, he was, nevertheless, widely read in the field of Church history. During the five years he served as secretary to Bishop John Hughes (1848–1853), he became interested in American Church history. He published his first volume in this field: *A Brief Sketch of the Early History of the Catholic Church on the Island of New York* (New York, 1853), which he later (1874) revised and enlarged. Bayley's volume is still an authoritative work for the history of the archdiocese. Its chief merit is in the rare sources Bayley had at his command when he undertook the study. While on his way to Europe in 1847, after having resigned the see of Vincennes, Bishop De LaHailandière left with Bishop Hughes a large collection of original letters and documents on early American Catholic history. This material Bayley used in his *Brief Sketch* and it was also from this valuable material that he published his *Memoirs of the Right Reverend Simon William Gabriel Bruté, D.D., First Bishop of Vincennes, with Sketches Describing His Recollections of Scenes Connected with the French Revolution and Extracts from His Journal* (New York, 1876). This latter work, undertaken twenty-three years after his first effort at historical writing, shows a considerable advance in historical technique.[8]

Of all the Catholic writers who attempted to write biography in the third quarter of the nineteenth century, perhaps the most successful was John R. G. Hassard (1836–1888). A convert to Catholicism in 1851, Hassard distinguished himself in the fields of journalism and literature, becoming in 1865 editor of the newly established *Catholic World* to which he contributed many essays and reviews. For a time he served as personal secretary to Archbishop John Hughes and within two years of the prelate's death he published his *Life of the Most Rev. John Hughes, D.D., First Archbishop of New York* (New York, 1866).[9] Having access to the correspondence of Hughes, Hassard made full use of it. He possessed a shrewd understanding of his subject, the problems he had to solve and the conflicts he had to face as well as the services he rendered to the Church; and with the aid of a facile pen he contributed to early Catholic historiography a readable and authoritative study.

In the last quarter of the nineteenth century and the first two decades of the twentieth there was a large group of scholarly Catholic writers who revealed that they had an appreciation of the modern critical method, although unable to avail themselves of the European training which their fellow-workers in the field of American history were using to advantage. The most distinguished of these writers who wrote before the turn of the century were Maes, O'Connell, Webb, Moosmueller, Lambing and Alerding.

Paul Camillus Maes (1846–1915), a Belgian by birth and educated in the seminaries of Roulers and Bruges and in the Ameri-

---

[8] Cf. Peter Guilday, "James Roosevelt Bayley," *Dictionary of American Biography,* II, 73-74.

[9] Richard J. Purcell, "John Rose Greene Hassard," *Dictionary of American Biography,* VIII, 382-383.

can College at Louvain, was ordained to the priesthood in 1868. Impressed by the need of American bishops for missionaries, he joined the diocese of Detroit where he labored zealously until 1885 when he was named bishop of Covington, Kentucky. Maes' contributions to American Catholic historiography fall within the period 1868–1885. While stationed in Monroe, Michigan (1871–1880) he wrote a brochure, *History of the Catholic Church in Monroe City and County,* printed in part in the *United States Catholic Historical Magazine,* April, 1888. This study showed promise of ability in historical writing and research, but it was not until he published his *Life of Rev. Charles Nerinckx, with a Chapter on the Early Catholic Missions in Kentucky* (Cincinnati, 1880) that he firmly established himself in the field of American Catholic historiography.[10]

Maes was painstaking and judicious in collecting the materials for this volume, seeking the help of the leading Catholic scholars of the period, including Shea and Bayley. It was only after years spent in collecting materials in the West, where Nerinckx labored so long and zealously; in Baltimore, where the Belgian missionary's letters to Archbishop John Carroll gave a mine of information as to his work, his trials and difficulties; and in Belgium, where Nerinckx had been known and respected for years previous to his arrival in America, that Maes began to write. In his Preface he reveals the efforts he made to produce an accurate history.

> At first writing, many misgivings natural to literary infancy, and increased not a little by necessary translations from the Latin, Flemish and French, halted me at every step. Besides, many gaps, filled, in some instances, only two or three years later, occurred in the narrative of events. I was continually cramped in its redaction, by lack of trustworthy information. This necessitated lengthy and often sterile researches, in rubbish-covered by-paths in the almost untrodden historical field of the end of the last and the beginning of the present century. Stray ends of information, gath-

---

[10] *Id.,* "Paul Camillus Maes," *Dictionary of American Biography,* XII, 193–194.

ered in out of the way places, have thus, at odd times,
been knotted together, in one unbroken skein of disen-
tangled strands. Hence, the reader must not always
expect the uneven thread of my narrative to smoothly
reel from the literary spindle.[11]

Concerning the thoroughness of his researches, he has to say:

The learned Archbishop Spalding has, it is true, elo-
quently embalmed Rev. Nerinckx' memory in the interesting pages of his *Sketches of Kentucky,* and from
them we have freely drawn. But we have succeeded in
obtaining many valuable and hitherto unpublished documents, which enable us to give a fuller history of the
venerable missionary's laborious career.

We can vouch for the historical accuracy of the details
of our narrative. We got them all at authentic sources,
more especially from letters of Rev. Father Nerinckx,
many of whose autographs the writer has in his possession. The few details we have about his ministry in
Belgium, we partly glean from his own letters, partly
from the *London Catholic Miscellany,* for April, 1825,
which obtained its information from Rev. John H.
Nerinckx, a brother of the missionary, living in London
at this time. From a Flemish narrative edited by J. G.
Lesage Ten Broek, at Amsterdam, in 1819, and one of
Father Nerinckx' letters, published by the same at
's Grovenshage in 1825, for the benefit of " the American missions," we gleaned many incidents of travel, and
some historical data not to be found elsewhere.[12]

Maes also used the records of the Hospital of Dendermonde,
Belgium; precious collection of manuscript letters, in the library
of the Bollandist Fathers, Brussels; and Nerinckx' manuscript
letters in the metropolitan archives.

Joseph Jeremiah O'Connell (1821–1894) was a Benedictine
connected with Belmont Abbey and a pioneer missionary in the
Carolinas and Georgia. After more than a quarter of a century
on this mission, O'Connell wrote not only a memoir of his own
life but also a comprehensive history of the Catholic Church in

---

[11] Camillus P. Maes, *Nerinckx,* v.

[12] *Ibid.,* vi–vii.

this area. Entitling it *Catholicity in the Carolinas and Georgia: Leaves of Its History: 1820–1878* (New York, 1879), he refused to call it a history because it lacked fullness of detail. " Most of the records of the diocese perished with the *United States Catholic Miscellany* in the conflagration of Charleston; the parochial registers were, in some instances, destroyed during the Civil War." [13]

The aim of O'Connell's work was to describe the establishment of Catholicism in the Carolinas and Georgia; the formation of missions, churches, and institutes; the privations, sufferings and fidelity of the early priests; and the first Catholics who were benefactors to religion and conspicuous for their piety. Into the narrative, O'Connell incorporated moral reflections and doctrinal explanations " That the reader may acquire a knowledge of the Faith while perusing a chapter of its history," thereby weakening the work considerably as a history. The whole volume centers around O'Connell's labors on the mission and is partially autobiographical. Diligent in collecting his materials, he produced an attractive study, and preserved considerable data for future studies on this sector of the Church's history.

A better known figure than O'Connell in this field of historical writing was Benjamin J. Webb. Webb had been for half a century in close contact with the Catholic traditions in Kentucky. He was born and reared in that State. In his youth and early manhood, he was on terms of intimate acquaintance with the leading pioneers, the story of whose lives and labors he was eventually to relate. As a publisher and later editor of the first Catholic paper in Kentucky, he had exceptional opportunities for acquiring knowledge not generally accessible to the public. His terms of service in the Senate of Kentucky greatly enlarged the circle of his acquaintance. As editor of the *Guardian* and *Catholic Advocate,* he acquired an easy and graceful style which is a marked characteristic of his single contribution to American Catholic historical writing. Encouraged by the clergy of Kentucky to write the history of Catholicism in that State, Webb undertook the task with diffidence. He spent seven years gath-

---

[13] Joseph J. O'Connell, *Catholicity in the Carolinas and Georgia,* x.

ering the data, and finally, after many difficulties and discouragements, he published 594 closely printed pages on *The Centenary of Catholicity in Kentucky* (Louisville, 1884).

Like his contemporaries, Webb was primarily interested in preserving all the facts that might be important. Lacking skill in interpretation and organization, he occasionally allowed the work to dwindle down to a mere chronicle of names of early Catholic settlers. The most serious objection to the book is the lack of organization. He followed a chronological order of events, particularly in the early chapters, but frequently interrupted with biographical sketches of noteworthy characters, thus drawing the reader away from the story. The result is a series of sketches and biographies, many of them admirably done, but detached from the thread of the general narrative. Despite these defects, Webb's contribution compares favorably with the studies of the other writers of this period.

Oswald Moosmueller, O.S.B., (1832-1901) was the pioneer historian of the Benedictine Order in the United States. The son of a wealthy family at Aidling in the Bavarian Alps, he received his early training in the old Benedictine College of Metten in the diocese of Ratisbon. Entering the Benedictine Order, he was sent at the end of his novitiate in 1852 to St. Vincent's Abbey at Latrobe, Pennsylvania. There he was ordained to the priesthood in 1856 by Bishop Michael O'Connor. After his ordination, he assisted at the mission in Carrolltown, Pennsylvania, at Holy Trinity Church, Brooklyn, New York, and St. Joseph's Church, Covington, Kentucky. In 1859 he went to Rio de Janeiro as a missionary to the newly arrived Germans and as a supervisor of the Benedictine program of agricultural and trade schools in Brazil. After two years, he was transferred to Sandwich, Ontario, as superior of the Benedictine monastery there. In 1863, he commenced a term of three years as prior of St. Mary's in Newark, New Jersey, and was then named procurator of the American Congregation and director of St. Elizabeth Seminary in Rome. He returned to America in 1872 and served as prior and treasurer of St. Vincent's Abbey, 1872-1874. He was superior of St. Benedict's Abbey in Atchison, 1874-1877, where he also acted as army chaplain and ministered among the Indians; and as superior of a colony of Benedictines who were working among the Negroes in Alabama and Georgia. In 1892, he was selected to organize the monastery of Cluny at Wetang, Illinois, where he remained until his death in 1901.[14]

Moosmueller began his literary activity in 1867 with a number of articles on the school question in *Katholische Volkszeitung.* These were followed in 1869 by some thirty sketches on " America Before Columbus " in the Cincinnati *Wahrheitsfreund,* which were later published as *Europaer in America vor Columbus* (Regensburg, 1879). Two years later, 1871, his first contribution in book form to American Church historiography came with the publication of his *St. Vincenz in Pennsylvania* (New York, 1891). Relying principally upon oral tradition and the archives of the Abbey as his sources, Moosmueller composed an authoritative work of some 384 pages. Although the researches of Griffin, Shea and Lambing have disproved some of the conclusions in his book, it remains a valuable contribution on the history of Catholicism in Western Pennsylvania.

Moosmueller's best historical work was perhaps his *Europaer in America vor Columbus.* It was one of the most important contributions that had yet been made to the Church history of Iceland, Greenland and Vinland. In many respects it was a daring work and showed signs of minute research.[15] Father Peter De Roo, in his *History of America Before Columbus* (2 vols., New York, 1900), cites it frequently. The success that the publication enjoyed encouraged Moosmueller to attempt the founding of an historical magazine which he called *Der Geschichtsfreund.* The purpose of the journal was to encourage the study of the history of the American Indian within the United States and to make

---

[14] Felix Fellner, "Oswald Moosmueller, the Pioneer Benedictine Historian of the United States," *Records,* XXXIV (1923), 1–16. Cf. Richard J. Purcell, "Oswald William Moosmueller," *Dictionary of American Biography,* XIII, 148–149.

[15] In his nineteenth chapter, Moosmueller endeavors to show that Benedictine monasteries existed in the New England States during the twelfth century, although he admits that no evident proofs exist.

known the apostolic labors of the Spanish and French missionaries. The publication lasted only two years (1882–1884).

In 1884, when Cardinal Bartolini extended an invitation to
Abbot Boniface Wimmer to send one of his monks to Rome to
assist in historical researches concerning the Church in America,
Moosmueller was the logical choice. In his reply to the Abbot's
letter offering him the position, Dom Oswold showed how well he
understood the qualities of a good historian:

> Your favor of the 18th inst. received in due time and
> I thank you for the compliment however undeserved on
> my part. Of those whom you may appoint for that po-
> sition, it will be expected that they are well acquainted
> with the literature of the history of America especially
> those learned works which were published during the
> 16th, 17th and 18th centuries. Without a thorough
> knowledge of these no man will be able to correct and
> refute all the errors and falsifications of Prescott, Ban-
> croft, Bishop Stephen Goodrich, etc. Not the his-
> torian-ambassador Bancroft, but the bookseller of that
> name in California collected a large library of the
> above-mentioned works and has already translated into
> English, in fact his five volumes under the title *The Na-
> tive Races of the Pacific States* are nothing else but
> translations of the Spanish works of Gargilasos, Clavi-
> gero, etc., published 200 years ago. When I read his
> first volume I remembered that I have in my MSS. ex-
> tracts from the original works which I (had) studied
> for my book *Europaer in America vor Columbus* and
> *Ueber die Abstammung der Indianer* in the first volume
> of the *Geschichtsfreund*. The principal reason why I
> cannot accept such a position is my deficiency in diplo-
> matics which is indispensable for an historian. At least
> one must have studied Mabillon's work *De re diplomatica*
> in 3 folio volumes to be able to read the Manuscripts and
> to judge them.[16]

A chair in history at The Catholic University of America
was offered to Moosmueller, but this he also declined. In 1889,

---

[16] Fellner, *loc. cit.*, 11–12. Although all of Moosmueller's publications
except his *Manual of Good Manners* (1874) were written in German,
nearly all of his correspondence with his superior is in English.

he published his most popular work: *Erzabt Bonifaz Wimmer,* a biography of his former superior. This book was selected by the editors of the *Wahrheitsfreund* as a premium for their readers and it reached a wide reading public. Moosmueller's position at the time he wrote the work as prior of St. Vincent's Abbey and archivist of the monastery gave him access to all the documents, particularly Abbot Wimmer's rich correspondence, for the preparation of an authoritative volume.

An outstanding figure in this particular group of American Catholic historians was Monsignor Andrew Arnold Lambing (1842–1918). Born in comparative poverty, Lambing as a youth began to earn his living on the farm. Subsequent employment in a brick yard and oil refinery produced a man of exceptional robustness. His formal education began at the age of twenty-one when he entered St. Michael's Seminary, Pittsburgh. In 1869 he was ordained to the priesthood and held the following pastorates in Pennsylvania: Loretto, 1869; Cameron Bottom, 1870; Kittanning, 1870–1873; Pittsburgh (St. Paul's Orphan Asylum and Church of St. Mary of Mercy), 1873–1885; and Wilkinsburg, 1885–1918.[17] Lambing definitely entered the field of historical study and writing shortly after 1877. In 1879 he attempted to organize a Catholic historical society but did not succeed.[18] The following year he published *A History of the Catholic Church in the Dioceses of Pittsburgh and Allegheny from Its Establishment to the Present Time* (New York, 1880). It was in this work that Lambing gave abundant evidence of the historical method which at once placed it apart from all that preceded him in the difficult field of diocesan history. It has been noted [19] that in one respect his method approached more closely contemporary scholarship than does the work of Shea, namely, in the critical essay on the sources which he included in his work. He likewise disclosed the difficulties that beset the plan

---

[17] George N. Shuster, "Andrew Arnold Lambing," *Dictionary of American Biography,* X, 559–560.

[18] See p. 37.

[19] Peter Guilday, "Lambing, Historian of Pittsburgh," *America,* L (December 16, 1933), 251–252.

of his history thereby enabling later students to estimate the value of the work with stricter accuracy:

> As regards the plan of the work, some difficulty 'was found in hitting upon the one that would be least open to objection; for while Catholicity was introduced from the East, the episcopal see that would seem to be the starting point was established in the West. The following is the plan adopted. After laying a general foundation of civil history, as briefly as possible, the manner in which the first Catholics came and the places where they settled are pointed out. This history of Pittsburgh is then taken up. The history of the Cathedral is made to some extent an epitome of that of the diocese. After it come the churches of Pittsburgh and Allegheny City and Allegheny County. Then, as the best way of returning to the East to sketch the early settlements, the counties lying on the southern boundary of the State, in which the Catholic population is small, are taken up from West to East. From that point a more natural return is made to the West by the northern and central counties. The religious orders and educational and charitable institutions close the work. Obituary notices of priests are inserted in the history of the church in which they last served, and at the time of their death.[20]

Five years later, Lambing published *The Baptismal Register of Fort Duquesne, 1754–1756* (Pittsburgh, 1885), which he translated from the French, adding to it an introductory essay and many valuable notes. Besides having the distinction of preparing the first diocesan history according to the principles of the genetic school of historical scholarship, Lambing also founded the first Catholic historical society in the United States and began the first Catholic historical quarterly.[21]

Lambing's next significant contribution to American Catholic historiography came in 1912, when he published his *Foundation Stones of a Great Diocese: Brief Biographical Sketches of the Deceased Bishops and Priests Who Labored in the Diocese of*

---

[20] Andrew Lambing, *A History of the Catholic Church in the Dioceses of Pittsburgh and Allegheny* (New York, 1880), 7.

[21] See p. 37.

*Pittsburgh from the Earliest Times to the Present* (New York, 1912). This was written to satisfy the request of his bishop and the clergy for a revision of his history of the diocese. He fully realized the amount of new material that had been discovered since the first publication and because of his advanced age and the cares of a large parish he felt himself unequal to the task. As it was, he did not have sufficient funds to publish *Foundation Stones of a Great Diocese,* and the volume had to be put through the press at the expense of the diocese. Another highly valuable historical study by Lambing was a small brochure entitled *Brief Sketch of St. James' Roman Catholic Church, Wilkinsburg, Pa.* (n.p., n.d.). In 1915, in recognition of his many services to the Church, Lambing was made a domestic prelate. During his lifetime he had a remarkably large acquaintance among non-Catholics, mostly business and professional men, and exercised a wide influence in civic affairs. He became the friend of Andrew Carnegie, who made him one of the trustees of his heavily endowed Carnegie Institute, and then of the Carnegie Institute of Technology. Historiographically, Lambing's greatest contribution was the patience and thoroughness with which he gathered together the raw materials of history. He displayed great skill in collecting the scattered sources of Catholic history and presenting them in a scientific manner with a high degree of accuracy.

In 1883, Herman Joseph Alerding (1845–1924) accomplished for the diocese of Vincennes what Lambing had done for the diocese of Pittsburgh. Born in Westphalia, Germany, Alerding came to America when a youth and received his ecclesiastical training in St. Gabriel's Seminary, Vincennes, Indiana; St. Thomas Seminary, Bardstown, Kentucky; and St. Meinrad's Seminary, St. Meinard, Indiana. Ordained in 1869, Father Alerding was engaged in pastoral work in the diocese of Vincennes until his appointment to the see of Fort Wayne, Indiana, in 1900. While engaged in his manifold pastoral duties he undertook, after years of patient research, the writing of a history of the diocese. His sole object in undertaking a work of this type was to preserve the documentary material that was rapidly perishing. His volume *A History of the Catholic Church in the Dio-*

*cese of Vincennes* (Indianapolis, 1883) has been described by Shea as a creditable, well-planned and well-arranged book.[22]

Since the field of diocesan history had not attracted many scholars before the turn of the century, Alerding's contribution was valuable not only from the standpoint of preservation of materials but also for its methodology. He divided the book into four parts: (1) sketches of the history of the diocese; (2) sketches of its series of bishops; (3) notices of the more prominent religious communities laboring in the diocese; and (4) biographical sketches of the priests and accounts of the principal institutions. In 1907, Alerding made a similar contribution for the diocese of Fort Wayne, *The Diocese of Fort Wayne, 1857 to September 22, 1907. A Book of Historical Reference. 1669–1907* (Fort Wayne, 1907).

The ventures of Lambing and Alerding into the field of diocesan history emphasized the need of more minute specialization before definitive histories of this type could be written. The beginning of the growth of Catholic historical societies in 1884 ushered in this new phase of American Catholic historiography. The societies brought together the leading Catholic historical scholars and, through the medium of their periodicals, many learned articles of a necessarily specialized nature made their appearance. These periodicals brought to the foreground many lesser-known but, nevertheless, capable historians. The writers who were the pioneers of this new development in American Catholic historiography were the early members of the two oldest Catholic historical societies in the United States, the American Catholic Historical Society of Philadelphia and the United States Catholic Historical Society of New York.[23] For a short period of time, all of them had the advantage of working in close conjunction with Shea whose influence was paramount. As he had drawn Parkman and other historians to the study of the labors of the early Catholic missionaries, Shea also brought about among his fellow-workers a distinct awakening of interest

---

[22] See Shea's review of the book in *Freeman's Journal,* Jan. 26 and Feb. 2, 1884.

[23] See pp. 39–43.

in many comparatively neglected fields of American Church history. The more prominent scholars of these two societies left few aspects of historical investigation untouched. The historical studies of this group of men, however, must be judged as pioneer efforts, carried through without the formal training and academic preparation which modern research demands. They are, therefore, faulty, but nevertheless important and useful as first digests of the records.

Richard Henry Clarke (1827-1911) was a New York lawyer who assisted John Gilmary Shea in the founding of the United States Catholic Historical Society in 1884. As early as 1872, Clarke made a careful historical study of the hierarchy in the United States which he published in that year in two volumes: *Lives of the Deceased Bishops of the Catholic Church in the United States* (New York, 1872). These volumes were favorably received and in 1888, two years after Shea had published his one volume on *The Hierarchy of the Catholic Church in the United States*, Clarke brought out a revised, enlarged and corrected edition in three volumes: *Lives of the Deceased Bishops of the Catholic Church in the United States* (New York, 1888). The work furnished a panoramic view of the history of Catholicism in the United States and of the part performed by each of the deceased prelates in extending and building up the Church. On the strength of this special study, Clarke published a *History of the Catholic Church in the United States from the Earliest Period to the Present Time, with Biographical Sketches of the Living Bishops* (Philadelphia, 1889-1890).

Besides these contributions to episcopology, Clarke wrote numerous articles of historical value for the various Catholic periodicals. His later studies include: " Catholic Protectories and Reformatories; " [24] " Our Converts; " [25] " A Noted Pioneer Convert of New England: Rev. John Thayer, 1758-1815; " [26] " Dominick Lynch; " [27] and " Catholic Life in New York City." [28]

[24] *American Catholic Quarterly Review,* XX (1895), 607-640.
[25] *Ibid.,* XVIII (1893), 539-561; XIX (1894), 112-138.
[26] *Ibid.,* XXIX (1904), 138-166.
[27] *American Catholic Historical Researches,* V (1888), 73-78.
[28] *Catholic World* (1898), 192-218.

Another industrious scholar in the United States Catholic Historical Society was Marc F. Vallette. Although his publications are not nearly so numerous as those of some of the other members, the interest he showed in the advancement of Catholic historical scholarship and the services he rendered in keeping the United States Catholic Historical Society in existence during its lean years, merit attention. Vallette's chief contribution is his " Sketch of Catholicity in Pennsylvania," (to 1844) which appeared in the *Catholic Record*.[29] This study was the result of original research and was used by Lambing and other historians in that field.

Archbishop Michael Augustine Corrigan of New York and Bishop Owen Bernard Corrigan of Baltimore were also vitally interested in the advancement of historical research and in particular in the success of the United States Catholic Historical Society. Archbishop Corrigan (1839–1902) in an effort to keep the society active contributed to its *Historical Records and Studies* two papers of historical value. The first was on " The Catholic Cemeteries of New York; " [30] and the other a " Register of the Clergy Laboring in the Archdiocese of New York from Early Missionary Times to 1885." [31]

Bishop Corrigan (1849–1929), late auxiliary bishop of Baltimore, is perhaps best remembered for his excellent work on the *History of the Catholic Schools in the Archdiocese of Baltimore* (Baltimore, 1924). But the studies that first earned him a place in American Catholic historiography were all centered on the history of the hierarchy of the United States. He attempted to provide a partial supplement to Reuss' work when he published the following series: " Chronology of the Catholic Hierarchy in

---

[29] XII (April, 1877), 321–328; XIII (July, 1877), 129–141; XIV (n.m. 1877), 210–222.

[30] *Historical Records and Studies,* I, pt. 2 (1900), 369–378.

[31] *Ibid.,* I, pt. 1 (1899), 18–44; pt. 2 (1900), 191–217; II, pt. 1 (1900), 36–81; pt. 2 (1901), 227–267; III, pt. 2 (1904), 288–319; IV, pt. 2 (1906), 96–138; V, pt. 1 (1907), 48–185; pt. 2 (1909), 392–413; VI, pt. 1 (1911), 36–57; pt. 2 (1912), 166–201; VII (1914), 198–205; VIII (1915), 229–244; IX (1916), 200–202.

the United States;"[32] "Episcopal Succession in the United States;"[33] "Rise of the Hierarchy in the United States;"[34] "Chronology of the Catholic Hierarchy in the United States;"[35] "Chronology of the American Hierarchy;"[36] "The Hierarchy in Our Colonial Possessions;"[37] "Titular Sees of the American Hierarchy;"[38] and "Chronological List Showing the Dates of Appointment of the Bishops of the United States."[39] Two other valuable pieces of research were on the Church in Maryland: "A Model Country Parish and Its Records,"[40] and "Catholicity in Allegany and Garrett Counties, Maryland."[41]

Francis X. Reuss (1847–1905) was a scholar associated with the American Catholic Historical Society. He was one of the first Catholic historians to enter the field of American episcopology. His *Biographical Cyclopedia of the Catholic Hierarchy of the United States, 1789–1898* (Milwaukee, 1898) represented eight years of untiring research during his leisure hours. To gather every possible bit of information, Reuss sent out over four thousand letters to various people. He tells us in the preface of his volume "No possible source of information has been overlooked; and so careful have I been to note the result in each case that I have even specially marked the places where it will be useless to search hereafter."[42] In spite of his thoroughness, the work is not without inaccuracies in the spelling of names, in dates and in references. Although it is of no value for data on the bishops who have been consecrated since 1897, it is still indispensable to the historian because of the rich material Reuss has gathered into his footnotes.

---

[32] *Catholic Historical Review*, I (Jan., 1916), 367–389.
[33] *Ibid.*, II (July, 1916), 127–145.
[34] *Ibid.*, II (Oct., 1916), 283–301.
[35] *Ibid.*, III (April, 1917), 22–32.
[36] *Ibid.*, III (July, 1917), 151–164.
[37] *Ibid.*, IV (April, 1918), 80–83.
[38] *Ibid.*, VI (Oct., 1920), 322–330.
[39] *Records*, XXXV (1924), 295–324.
[40] *Ibid.*, 197–241.
[41] *Ibid.*, XXXVI (1925), 113-154, 209–253.
[42] Reuss, *op. cit.*, iii.

A list of Reuss' contributions to the historical journals of his day would require several pages. He was a prolific writer and much of what he contributed was really spade work in the sources. His studies on " St. Peter's Church, Columbia, Lancaster Co., Pa.; " [43] " Some Recollections of Reverend Patrick Rafferty, Missionary of the Diocese of Philadelphia, 1791–1821– 1863; " [44] and " Catholic Chronicles of Lancaster County, Pennsylvania," [45] are important for the early history of the Church in that State.

Of the group of writers who pioneered in the development of the historical societies and in specialized research, the outstanding figures were Lawrence F. Flick, Martin I. J. Griffin, Thomas C. Middleton, O.S.A., and Charles G. Herbermann.

Lawrence F. Flick (1856–1938) won wide recognition as a tuberculosis specialist and a Catholic historian. Receiving his early education from the Benedictines in Pennsylvania, he later obtained his medical degree from Jefferson Medical College. After effecting a complete cure on himself for tuberculosis, he specialized in preventive medicine, particularly in the pathology and treatment of tuberculosis. Besides writing many papers on the disease, Flick contributed three books to the literature: *Consumption, a Curable and Preventable Disease, What the Layman Should Know About It* (New York, 1903), *The Development of Our Knowledge of Tuberculosis* (New York, 1925) and *Tuberculosis* (New York, 1937).[46] Another absorbing interest of Flick's was the history and development of Catholicism in the United States. He was one of the founders of the American Catholic Historical Society in 1884 and of the American Catholic Historical Association in 1919, of which he was the first of a long line of distinguished presidents. From 1893 to 1896 and again in 1913–1914, Flick served as president of the American Catholic Historical Society. He was a man of precise habits, and the papers he contributed to the field of American Catholic history

---

[43] *Records*, IV (1893), 90–124.
[44] *Ibid.*, VIII (1897), 394–398.
[45] *Ibid.*, XVIII (1907), 354–361.
[46] *National Cyclopedia of American Biography*, XXVIII, 434–435.

give abundant evidence of careful research. Among his best known studies in Catholic Church history are: " Biographical Sketch of Rev. Henry Lemke, O.S.B., 1796–1882;" [47] " Mathias James O'Conway, Philologist, Lexicographer and Interpreter of Languages, 1766–1842;" [48] " The French Refugee Trappists in the United States;" [49] " Samuel Castner, Jr.;" [50] and " Gallitzin." [51]

Closely associated with Flick in investigating the history of the Church in Pennsylvania and Maryland was Martin I. J. Griffin (1842–1911). One of the leading journalists and historians of that period, Griffin was very early in life associated with various Catholic publications as contributor and editor. In 1872, he was appointed secretary of the Irish Catholic Benevolent Union, founding and editing its official organ, the *Irish Catholic Benevolent Union Journal,* commonly called the *ICBU Journal.* Shortly after this, he founded and edited *Griffin's Journal.* His articles on local Catholic history printed in this latter periodical eventually led to the founding of the American Catholic Historical Society of Philadelphia on July 22, 1884. [52] In January, 1887, he began the publication of *The American Catholic Historical Researches,* which he edited until his death in 1911. During the years of his study of the records of American Catholic history, Griffin collected from every available source a large amount of original data that has been of much value and assistance to the historians of the development of the Church in the United States. Most of the material he so perseveringly gathered he made available to future scholars in the volumes of the *Researches.* His most important publications include a *History of Commodore John Barry* (Philadelphia, 1903), and *Catholics and the American Revolution* (3 vols., Ridley Park, Pennsylvania, 1907–1911).

In the numerous articles he contributed to the various historical journals there are preserved many details, otherwise neglected, of

---

[47] *Records,* IX (1898), 129–192.
[48] *Ibid.,* X (1899), 257–299, 385–422; XI (1900), 9–32, 156–176.
[49] *Ibid.,* I (1884–1886), 86–116.
[50] *Ibid.,* XL (1929), 193–225.
[51] *Catholic Historical Review,* XIII (Oct., 1927), 394–469.
[52] See p. 39.

early Catholic life. These include his "History of the Rt. Rev. Michael Egan, D.D., First Bishop of Philadelphia;"[53] "Thomas FitzSimons, Pennsylvania's Catholic Signer of the Constitution;"[54] "Life of Bishop Conwell of Philadelphia," revised and edited by the Rev. Lemuel B. Norton[55] as well as his numerous studies on several Philadelphia churches which appeared in the *Records*.

Thomas C. Middleton, O.S.A., (1842–1923) was one of the outstanding writers of this group, making many important contributions to American Catholic historiography. Graduating from Villanova College in Pennsylvania in 1858, he entered the Italian novitiate at Tolentino and later studied at San Agostino in Rome. While making his theological studies he gained a reputation for scholarship and linguistic proficiency. Returning to Villanova College in 1865, he spent the remainder of his life there as a teacher, prefect of discipline, vice-rector, rector (1876–1881), associate provincial and secretary of the American province of the Augustinians (1878–1914), librarian and historiographer of the Order.

Middleton was one of the founders and the first president (1885–1890) of the American Catholic Historical Society and for many years the editor of the society's official organ, the *Records*. He devoted every spare moment from his official duties to a study of the history of his Order and to researches into the Catholic history of Pennsylvania, .and soon became a recognized authority in this field. Careful and persevering in his researches, Middleton delved into parish and local records and industriously prepared a voluminous manuscript of *notabilia* of community life from 1868–1923.[56] Middleton contributed numerous articles and

---

[53] *American Catholic Historical Researches,* IX (1892), 65–80, 113–128, 161–176; X (1893), 17–32, 81–96, 113–128, 161–192.

[54] *Ibid.,* V (1888), 2–27.

[55] *Records,* XXIV (1913), 16–42, 162–178, 217–250, 348–361; XXV (1914), 52–67, 146–178, 217–248, 296–341; XXVI (1915), 64–77, 131–165, 227–249; XXVII (1916), 74–87, 145–160, 275–283, 359–378; XXVIII (1917), 64–84, 150–183, 244–265, 310–347; XXIX (1918), 170–182, 250–261, 360–384.

[56] These are contained in two ledgers of 239 and 315 closely written

scrupulously exact abstracts from parochial registers to the *Records, American Catholic Historical Researches, American Catholic Quarterly Review* and the *Ecclesiastical Review.* His detailed accounts of the Church in Lansingburgh,[57] Mechanicsville,[58] Atlantic City, New Jersey [59] and of his native parish St. Mary's of Our Mother of Consolation, Chestnut Hill, Philadelphia,[60] are carefully prepared studies. Middleton's more serviceable monographic studies are his *Historical Sketch of Villanova, 1842–1892* (Philadelphia, 1893); *Directory of the Augustinians in the United States* (Villanova, Pennsylvania, 1909); and " A List of Catholic and Semi-Catholic Periodicals Published in the United States from the Earliest Date Down to the Close of the Year 1892," which appeared in the *Records.*[61]

The name of Charles G. Herbermann (1840–1916) is an important one in the annals of the United States Catholic Historical Society. Graduating from the Jesuit college of St. Francis Xavier in New York, he became a member of the faculty. This post he held for eleven years. In 1869, when only twenty-nine years old, he accepted a position on the faculty of the City College of New York. There he taught Latin and Latin Literature (1869–1914) and served as librarian (1873–1914). Herbermann's first important advance in American Catholic scholarship came in 1905, when he was chosen editor-in-chief of the *Catholic*

---

pages respectively. Cf. Richard J. Purcell, " Thomas Cooke Middleton," *Dictionary of American Biography,* XII, 603–604, and Francis E. Tourscher, " Fr. Thomas Cooke Middleton, D.D., O.S.A.," *Records,* XXXV (1924), 20–32.

[57] " An Old-Time Catholic Pioneer of Lansingburgh, N. Y. (A.D. 1767–1842)," *Records,* VII (1896), 1–26.

[58] " A Typical Old-Time Country Mission: St. Paul's of Mechanicsville, New York. From A.D. *ante* 1829–1908," *Records,* XIX (1908), 276–304, 361–384.

[59] " A New Jersey Sea-Side Mission. St. Nicholas of Tolentine's of the Augustinians at Atlantic City. A.D. 1855–1906," *Records,* XVII (1906), 67–85, 144–179.

[60] " Some Memoirs of Our Lady's Shrine at Chestnut Hill, Pennsylvania. A.D. 1855–1900," *Records,* XII (1901), 11–40, 129–168, 257–293, 385–418.

[61] IV (1893), 213–242; XIX (1908), 18–41.

*Encyclopedia,* a post which he held until the completion of the monumental work in 1914. As editor, he contributed many excellent articles to the volumes. His association with the United States Catholic Historical Society was fortunate, since it was under his leadership that the society took on new life and began to show important results.[62] Nine volumes of the society's quarterly *Historical Records and Studies* appeared under his editorship and set a high standard in American Catholic historiography. The more serviceable studies Herbermann himself contributed to this journal include: " The Rt. Rev. John Dubois, D.D., Third Bishop of New York; "[63] Rt. Rev. Winand Michael Wigger, D.D., Third Bishop of Newark; "[64] " A French Emigré Colony in the United States (1789–1793); "[65] " John James Maximilian Oertel; "[66] " John A. Mooney and His Literary Work; "[67] " Reverend Andrew Francis Monroe, S.J.; "[68] " Reverend Charles Hyppolite de Luynes, S.J.; "[69] and " Reverend Simon Fouché, S.J." [70] While engaged in research work in the library at Dunwoodie Seminary, he became interested in the history of the Sulpicians. After a careful investigation of the sources, he published his best-known volume *The Sulpicians in the United States* (New York, 1916). This work he undertook late in life, when he was threatened with blindness which eventually came upon him. Because of partial blindness he was forced to dictate most of the work and many errors crept into it, keeping it from being a definitive study. It was, however, of sufficient worth to enhance the author's already established reputation.

---

[62] See pp. 42–44.

[63] *Historical Records and Studies,* I, pt. 2 (1900), 278–355.

[64] *Ibid.,* II, pt. 2 (1901), 292–320.

[65] *Ibid.,* I, pt. 1 (1899), 77–96,

[66] *Ibid.,* IV, pt. 1 (1906), 139–144.

[67] *Ibid.,* XIII (1919), 120–128.

[68] *Ibid.,* X (1917), 152–161.

[69] *Ibid.,* 130–151.

[70] *Ibid.,* IX (1916), 180–186.

# CHAPTER V

## HISTORIOGRAPHY OF THE AMERICAN CATHOLIC CHURCH: 1915-1943

ALTHOUGH the contemporary period in American Catholic historiography does not begin until after 1915, there were many evidences of its approach towards the end of the nineteenth century. Around 1895 a number of writers began to display characteristics of the more recent authors who have brought to their work all the resources of modern critical scholarship.[1] Of this

---

[1] Authors who contributed some excellent specimens of historical scholarship in the various fields of American Church history during this period included: a) In the field of provincial history: Michael J. Riordan who wrote the section entitled "Archdiocese and Province of Baltimore," for the third and final volume of *The Catholic Church in the United States of America* (1-239), a work undertaken to celebrate the golden jubilee of Pope Pius X but never completed; William Byrne, William Leahy and others who wrote the imposing *History of the Catholic Church in the New England States* (2 vols., Boston, 1899); Edwin V. O'Hara who compiled the *Pioneer Catholic History of Oregon* (2nd ed. enlarged, Portland, 1916); John Talbot Smith, *The Catholic Church in New York* (2 vols., New York, 1908); and James H. Defouri, the author of the *Historical Sketch of the Catholic Church in New Mexico* (San Francisco, 1887); b) In the field of diocesan history the more important contributions include: Michael J. Riordan's *Cathedral Records of Baltimore* (Baltimore, 1906); George F. Houck's *A History of Catholicity in Northern Ohio and in the Diocese of Cleveland from 1749 to December 31, 1900* (2 vols., Cleveland, 1903); Antoine I. Rezek's *History of the Diocese of Sault Ste. Marie and Marquette* (2 vols., Chicago, 1906-07); Francis J. Magri's *Catholic Church in the City and Diocese of Richmond* (Richmond, 1906); c) In the extensive field of parochial history important works include: Francis J. Hertkorn's *Retrospect of Holy Trinity Parish, Philadelphia, 1789-1914* (Philadelphia, 1914); Thomas F. Hopkins' *Historic Sketch of St. Mary's Church* (Charleston, 1898); Francis X. McGowan's *Historical Sketch of St. Augustine's Church, Philadelphia* (Philadelphia,

group of writers, William J. Howlett (1847–1936) illustrates best the transition that was gradually taking place. When Howlett began to write, sufficient preliminary work had been done on many aspects of American Catholic life to permit a new group of writers, equipped with modern historical methods, to sift the materials and prepare the way for more definitive writing. Howlett did not belong to this latter class, but in his writings characteristics of both groups are present.

Born in New York, he came with his parents to Cass County, in southern Michigan, at the age of six. Some ten years later, he migrated with them in a covered wagon to Colorado, arriving there in 1865. * In 1866 he began teaching in a Catholic school for boys in Denver and also began his seminary studies. These he continued in St. Thomas Seminary at Bardstown, Kentucky (1868–1869). He later went to Paris where he took his philosophy and theology and was ordained in 1876. From 1877 to 1913, he served on the mission in Colorado, and from 1913 to his death in 1936, he was Chaplain of Loretto Motherhouse, Nerinckx, Kentucky.[2]

As was the case with the majority of Catholic historians of his era, William Howlett's literary activity was largely incidental to his more active ministry in behalf of souls. Most of his research was carried on in spare moments between pressing duties. The greater part of his historical studies are concerned with the annals of Catholic life in Kentucky. The first volume of importance from his pen was his *Historical Tribute to St. Thomas Seminary at Poplar Neck Near Bardstown, Kentucky* (St. Louis, 1906). In his *Recollections* concerning the circumstances attend-

---

1891) ; d) In the field of religious historiography, the following give evidence of the scientific approach: George F. Lathrop's *Annals of the Georgetown Convent of the Visitation* (Cambridge, Mass., 1893) ; Anna B. McGill's *Sisters of Charity of Nazareth, Kentucky* (New York, 1917) ; Anna C. Minogue's *Loretto, Annals of a Century* (New York, 1912) ; John F. Byrne's *Redemptorists in the United States* (Philadelphia, 1932) ; and Bonaventure Hammer's *Franziskaner in den Vereinigten Staaten* (Köln, 1892).

[2] Thomas F. O'Connor, "William Howlett, Pioneer Missionary and Historian," *Mid-America,* XX (1938), 103–106.

ing the writing of this work, he gives an insight into the motives governing some of his Kentucky investigations:

> It was my first visit since my seminary days, and it was a saddening visit. The grounds were there, the church was there, the log residence of Bishop Flaget was there, but not a sign of the seminary buildings remained except the excavation where our basement refectory once was. The grounds were strewn with logs, the church was in bad repair, and the whole had a dilapidated and neglected appearance. I wrote a letter on the condition of the place to the *Record* of Louisville and that letter did more than I anticipated. It aroused the spirit of the priests of Kentucky to the importance of preserving the ancient landmarks of their faith, and refreshing the memory of the present generation to the glories of the past. . . . The result was my book on the history of Saint Thomas' Seminary.[3]

This effort was not intended to be a definitive and detailed history of the pioneer institution, as he plainly indicates in his preface to the work:

> While securing historical permanence to the course of the oldest Seminary in the West, my intention has been rather to give definite form to the many expressions of affection and reverence for the old *Alma Mater* and those connected with it, to embody the general feelings of all old St. Thomas' students and to indicate the reasons for the universal good will.
> To do this, I have taken the more important incidents connected with the establishment of the Seminary, its internal working, and the special and lasting results that trace their causes to it. Minor matters of detail I have used to show the connection between the greater events and the unity of spirit and action that ran through the whole course of its existence.[4]

Howlett's best known and perhaps most ambitious project was his *Life and Times of the Right Reverend Joseph P. Machebeuf,*

---

[3] *Op. cit.,* 105.
[4] *Ibid.,* 5.

*D.D.* (Pueblo, Colorado, 1906). This volume was actually a history of the Catholic Church in Ohio, New Mexico and Colorado. Howlett had a twenty-four year acquaintance with this pioneer missionary and first bishop of Colorado. Years before he undertook the writing of the *Life,* he had advised Machebeuf's sister to preserve as sources the bishop's letters to his family in France; it is these letters that constitute the chief documentary source of the volume.[5] Although the work ranks with the better ecclesiastical biographies published in this period, Howlett did not have access to many supplementary sources which would have further enhanced the value of his book. This is true of all his projects. Although in some instances he shows evidence that he had access to many documentary materials, he was rarely in a position to undertake the intensive research necessary for a definitive study.

In 1915, there appeared the last of his important publications, the *Life of Rev. Charles Nerinckx, Pioneer Missionary of Kentucky and Founder of the Sisters of Loretto at the Foot of the Cross* (Techny, Illinois, 1915). In the foreword to this volume, Howlett gives indications of the new era in Catholic historiography:

> Several sketches and an extended biography of Father Nerinckx have been written, and the author of this volume would not disparage any of them. They have proven treasures of information for him, and he makes no secret of having made the most of them in the present work. The utility of a new biography comes from an aroused interest in our early church history, and a call for a closer grouping of events and men belonging to the same periods and movements.[6]

After the publication of this account of Father Nerinckx, Howlett's contributions to the history of the Church in the West took the form of shorter accounts of persons and institutions in periodicals and reviews. The more important of these were: "The Very Rev. Stephen Theodore Badin, Proto-priest of the

---

[5] O'Connor, *loc. cit.,* 106.
[6] P. ix.

United States;"[7] "St. Joseph's, the Cathedral Church of the Diocese of Bardstown, Kentucky;"[8] "The Early Days of St. Joseph's College at Bardstown, Kentucky;"[9] "A Fortuitous Find of Some Letters of Ira B. Dutton, the Brother Joseph of the Lepers of Molokai."[10]

Another link between the Catholic writers of the old school and those of the new is Father Victor Francis O'Daniel, O.P. (1868–    ). Unlike Howlett, however, he comes closer to the scholars who have been trained in the modern critical methods. Born and reared in Kentucky, O'Daniel's researches have mainly centered around the history of Catholicity in that State. For a long term of years he was professor of theology in Kentucky, in California, and in Washington, holding at the same time various educational offices in the Dominican Order. In 1911, he was appointed archivist of St. Joseph's Province and soon became recognized as the historiographer of the Order of Friars Preacher in the United States.

His career as an historian began with the creation of the *Catholic Historical Review* (1915), of which he was a co-founder and for many years an associate editor. It was in his scholarly contributions to this quarterly that O'Daniel first gave evidence that he belonged to the modern school of critical historical writers. Between 1915 and 1920, he contributed the following studies to the journal: "The Rev. John Ceslas Fenwick, O.P. (1759–1815);"[11] "The Right Rev. Richard Luke Concanon, O.P., the First Bishop of New York (1747–1810);"[12] "Concanon's Election to the See of New York (1808–10);"[13] "The Right Rev. Juan De Las Cabezas de Altamirano; the First Bishop to Visit the Present Territory of the United States (1562–1615);"[14] "Archbishop John Hughes, American Envoy

---

[7] *Historical Records and Studies,* IX (June, 1916), 141–146.
[8] *Illinois Catholic Historical Review,* IV (Jan., 1922), 278–285.
[9] *Ibid.,* 372–380.
[10] *Records,* XLII (1931), 367–378.
[11] *Catholic Historical Review,* I (April, 1915), 17–29.
[12] *Ibid.,* I (Jan., 1916), 400–421.
[13] *Ibid.,* II (April, 1916), 19–46.
[14] *Ibid.,* II (Jan., 1917), 400–414.

to France (1861); "[15] " The Centenary of Ohio's Oldest Catholic Church (1818–1918); "[16] " Cuthbert Fenwick—Pioneer Catholic and Legislator of Maryland; "[17] " Letter to the Reverend Peter Guilday "[18] in which he answers some queries anent the existence of an early ordinance prohibiting the erection of a Catholic church within the municipal limits of Cincinnati and the struggle of the first Catholics in the city; " Some Letters of Fathers Badin and Nerinckx to Bishop Carroll; "[19] " Fathers Badin and Nerinckx and the Dominicans in Kentucky; a Long Misunderstood Episode in American Church History." [20]

The first book O'Daniel published was *The Life of Very Rev. Charles Hyacinth McKenna, O.P., P.G., Missionary and Apostle of the Holy Name Society* (New York, 1917). It was on the merits of this volume that he firmly established himself in the modern school of critical scholars. Between 1920 and 1932, O'Daniel published no less than six volumes centering about the history of the Dominican Order in the United States. In 1920, he issued *The Right Rev. Edward Dominic Fenwick, O.P., Founder of the Dominicans in the United States, Pioneer Missionary in Kentucky, Apostle of Ohio, First Bishop of Cincinnati* (Washington, D. C., 1920). After this work, O'Daniel published the following studies at the rate of one volume every three years: *An American Apostle, the Very Reverend Matthew Anthony O'Brien, O.P., Model Priest and Religious Promoter of Catholic Education, Tireless and Fruitful Harvester of Souls in the United States and Canada* (Washington, D. C., 1923); *The Father of the Church in Tennessee; or, the Life, Times, and Character of the Right Reverend Richard Pius Miles, O.P., the First Bishop of Nashville* (Washington, D. C., 1926); *Dominicans in Early Florida* (New York, 1930) published as volume XII of the *Monograph Series* of the United States Catholic Historical Society; and *A Light of the Church in Kentucky; or, The*

---

[15] *Ibid.*, III (Oct., 1917), 336–339.

[16] *Ibid.*, IV (April, 1918), 18–37.

[17] *Ibid.*, V (July–Oct., 1919), 156–174.

[18] *Ibid.*, V (Jan., 1920), 428–435.

[19] *Ibid.*, VI (April, 1920), 66–88.

[20] *Ibid.*, 15–45.

*Life, Labors and Character of the Very Rev. Samuel Thomas Wilson . . . Pioneer Educator and First Provincial of a Religious Order in the United States* (Washington, D. C., 1932).

In the foreword to his life of Bishop Fenwick, O'Daniel reveals his attitude towards historical scholarship:

> Ever and always, the author has sought to base his narrative on bedrock, drawing the history of the friar prelate from only first-hand sources. The footnotes show but few instances in which he failed to accomplish this. Documents, however, especially if they are litigious or written with a view to gain a point, cannot always be taken at their face-value. For this reason, all documents were carefully studied in order to detect what was alloy of bias and prejudice, and what genuine historic truth. . . .
>
> Another effort that involved no little difficulty was that of making the narrative at once popular and scientific. We have sought to adapt the text of the story to the general public, for whom the book is principally written. The copious footnotes are largely intended to satisfy the demands of the scholar.[21]

O'Daniel's latest contribution to American Catholic historiography is his comprehensive study of the history of the province, entitled: *The Dominican Fathers of St. Joseph* (New York, 1942). This complete and detailed account of the labors of the Dominicans in the United States fittingly rounds out a sizeable library of Dominican history contributed by the only chronicler of note the Order has produced.

The contribution of Thomas O'Gorman (1843–1921) to the field of general literature in 1893 was of minor importance in the historiography of the American Church. O'Gorman received his education in France and was ordained in 1865. For a time he served as president of St. Thomas College in St. Paul, Minnesota. In 1890, he became the first occupant of the chair of Church history at the Catholic University of America, a position he held until 1896, when he was appointed bishop of Sioux Falls. His general survey of American Catholic history, written

---

[21] O'Daniel, *Fenwick*, xi–xii.

for Scribner's *American Church History Series* [22] was a compact volume entitled: *History of the Roman Catholic Church in the United States* (New York, 1895).

Although the work was well received, it was hardly more than a summary of Shea's four volumes. As a pioneer in compiling a single volume of a general history of the American Church, O'Gorman did not avoid making many errors and faulty interpretations. Despite these deficiencies, however, his effort was of value and by bringing the story of the Church's growth in the United States down to the year 1895, he gained for himself a place in American historiography.

The progenitor of the modern era of American Catholic historical scholarship was Thomas Hughes, S.J. (1849–1939). Born in England and educated at Stonyhurst, he joined the Missouri Province of the Jesuits at the age of seventeen, in order to consecrate his life to missionary work among the American Indians. However, after his ordination to the priesthood by Cardinal Gibbons in 1878, he was named professor of philosophy at Xavier University, Cincinnati, Ohio. Later he taught at St. Louis University and the University of Detroit. In 1893, his historical researches took him to Rome, where he remained until his death at the age of ninety, laboring first at the American College and later at the Gesu.

Hughes was a learned man and a careful scholar. Soon after his ordination to the priesthood, he was commissioned to share in the preparation of a comprehensive historical series giving an authentic account of the Society over the world. During the first century and a half of Jesuit work in the British colonies of North America, that mission was part of the English Province and not until after the beginning of the nineteenth century was a separate American Province established. Although Hughes was appointed historian of the American Province, he was also commissioned to write the history of the Jesuits in the English colonies. Hughes devoted himself to this task for over forty years,

---

[22] Published under the auspices of the American Society of Church History. Cf. Richard J. Purcell, "Thomas O'Gorman," *Dictionary of American Biography*, XIV, 3.

investigating most of the authorities and gathering all the documents of value. Between 1907 and 1917, he published the fruits of his research in four volumes, two of text and two of documents, entitled: *History of the Society of Jesus in North America, Colonial and Federal* (London, 1907–17). He was the first writer after Shea to display careful and exhaustive scholarship. In these volumes, Hughes showed the importance of writing history from the sources, for he gave more fully and more accurately than ever before the story of the faithful work of the early missionaries. For this reason these volumes have remained the standard history of the Jesuits in English-speaking America. In the course of his researches he unearthed a wealth of documentary material which threw new light on matters of general American history. For the use of all future scholars he gave, in Volume I of the text, a 138-page description of the source material; this includes sources, edited and unedited, as well as a history of the archives and the literature. Although Hughes did not write his text with complete impartiality, and his interpretation of events and personalities is at times unduly severe, no scholar of American history can neglect his volumes.

Contemporary with Hughes, and writing in the same field of American Church history, was the Franciscan Friar, Zephyrim Engelhardt (1851–1934). Born in Germany, he came with his parents to Kentucky in 1852. A year after his ordination, in 1878, he was sent as a missionary among the Menominee Indians at Keshena, Wisconsin. After serving a term as superior of the missions of northern Wisconsin, he worked among the Indians in Mendocino County, California. From 1900 until his death he lived at the Old Mission of Santa Barbara, California, devoting himself to research and writing on the history of the Franciscan, Jesuit, and Dominican Orders in the southwest.[23] Before his researches into missionary history, Engelhardt published a short biography of Catherine Tegakouita and a monthly magazine, *Anishinable Enamiad,* both in the language of the Ottawas.

As early as the year 1897, Engelhardt published his first book on mission history: *Franciscans in California* (Michigan, 1897).

---

[23] *National Cyclopedia of American Biography,* XXIV, 134–135.

This and his *Franciscans in Arizona* (Michigan, 1899) were the forerunners of his standard work on the subject: *Missions and Missionaries of California* (4 vols., San Francisco, 1908–1915).[24] This work Engelhardt continued in a series of monographs on the various local missions, namely: *San Diego Mission* (San Francisco, 1929); *San Luis Rey Mission* (San Francisco, 1921); *San Juan Capistrano Mission* (Los Angeles, Cal., 1922); *Santa Barbara Mission* (San Francisco, 1923); *San Francisco, or Mission Dolores* (Chicago, 1924); *San Fernando Rey* (Chicago, 1927); *San Gabriel Mission* (San Gabriel, Cal., 1927); *San Miguel Archangel* (Santa Barbara, Cal., 1929); *San Antonio de Padua* (Santa Barbara, Cal., 1929); *Nuestra Senora de la Soledad* (Santa Barbara, Cal., 1929); *San Buenaventura* (Santa Barbara, Cal., 1930); *Mission San Juan Bautista* (Santa Barbara, Cal., 1931); *Mission La Concepcion Purisima* (Santa Barbara, Cal., 1932); *Mission Santa Inez* (Santa Barbara, Cal., 1932); *Mission San Luis Obispo* (Santa Barbara, 1933); and *Mission San Carlos,* edited by Fr. Felix Pudlowski, O.F.M. (Santa Barbara, 1934).

Engelhardt's monumental work on the *Missions and Missionaries of California* was a detailed account of the vicissitudes of the Franciscans in the Californias. In this, as in all subsequent volumes, he spared no pains to make his work proof against errors of fact. He was one of the first Catholic writers to take issue with many of the statements of Hubert H. Bancroft, John S. Hittell, and other historians of California, particularly with reference to Father Junipero Serra and to the Jesuits before their expulsion from Lower California. To correct the misrepresentations of these men, who wrote their extensive histories of California during a period in the latter half of the nineteenth century that was almost militantly non-Catholic, Engelhardt delved into all the then known archival sources. One of the most valuable sections of his work is the critical essay on the sources of California mission history contained in his second volume.

Though some work of merit and permanent value was accomplished in the nineteenth century, several obstacles impeded the

---

24 A second edition was issued at Santa Barbara, California, 1929–1930.

growth of critical historical scholarship in Catholic circles. In the first place, the purpose behind most of the writings was two-fold: (1) to preserve as far as possible all the existing records; (2) to transmit them in such a way as to edify pious readers. Devotion to the Church made the early historians zealous for the safeguarding of its records and traditions; furthermore, the tendency was to write about the period close at hand and about the personalities whom they knew, with little thought of interpretation.

A second reason why Catholic historical study made no greater advance was the almost entire absence in its initial period of professionally-trained historians. Most of the Catholic chroniclers had taken up the study of Church history merely as a hobby. Almost all of them were busy professional men or priests, burdened with the care of extensive parishes. Their historical activity was largely incidental to the manifold duties demanded by their various professions or vocations. The difficulties the Catholic historical scholar had to face if he wished to pursue the science as a profession were clearly evident in the life of John Gilmary Shea.

A third factor, and perhaps the most important, was the complete lack of professional training in the historical sciences on the part of Catholic scholars. The renaissance that effectively marked nineteenth century American historiography was brought about by the introduction of European historical methods into the American universities. History became far more critical and the historians' attention was directed to the sources and the dependability of their data, rather than to the meaning and interpretation of the facts. This growing interest in method early manifested itself in the organization of historical seminars in the American universities. The first of these was established in 1869 by Charles K. Adams at Michigan [25] and the second by Henry Adams at Harvard in 1871.[26] The most fruitful of these

---

[25] Harry Elmer Barnes, *A History of Historical Writing* (Norman, Oklahoma, 1938), 260.

[26] James Truslow Adams maintains "it is . unquestionable that he [Henry Adams] was the first American teacher to introduce that method

seminars was that of Herbert Baxter Adams at Johns Hopkins University.[27]

All of these men had observed the work done in the seminars in the German universities of Berlin, Leipzig, Bonn, Göttingen, and Heidelberg, and the Sorbonne in Paris; and it was they who shaped the development of historical study and teaching before 1890.

The Johns Hopkins seminar had perhaps the most brilliant group of students, most of whom later became important in the academic world. So successful was Herbert B. Adams' seminar, that he began, in 1882, the issue of the Johns Hopkins University *Studies in Historical and Political Science.* This series was the first systematic publication of detailed historical studies in America.[28]

The seminar movement soon spread to other universities, and publication not only encouraged careful investigation but preserved the results for the use of others. At Yale, two seminars were inaugurated after the arrival of George B. Adams. In 1889–1890, Andrew D. White had established at Cornell eleven full courses of history, three of which were seminars. At Columbia, in 1880, John W. Burgess founded the School of Political Science with the first faculty of the University devoted to advanced non-professional research. By 1886, Columbia had started her *Political Science Quarterly,* and in 1891, her *Studies in History, Economics and Public Law.*[29]

As late as the second decade of the twentieth century, not one Catholic university in the country had a seminar in its department of history. American Catholic Church history was not given this dignity until 1915. In that year the first successful historical seminar was established by Dr. Peter Guilday at The Cath-

---

[seminar] into this country," "Henry Adams and the New Physics," *Yale Review,* n.s. XIX (1930), 285.

[27] Barnes, *op. cit.,* 259.

[28] John M. Vincent, "Herbert B. Adams," American Historical Association *Annual Report,* I, 1901 (Washington, D. C., 1902), 199.

[29] Ivy Faye Neds, "A Half Century of American Historiography, 1884–1934" (Doctoral thesis, Ohio State University, 1935), 10.

olic University of America, shortly after the conclusion of his studies at Louvain. At the same time he created the first great training school for Catholic historians in the United States. With the work of Guilday, the modern period of American Catholic historiography really begins in its fullest scientific sense.

Born in 1884, Guilday received his early education in the Catholic schools of Philadelphia. In 1907, he was sent to the University of Louvain in Belgium, where he was trained from 1907 to 1914 in the well-known history seminar of Alfred Canon Cauchie. His doctoral dissertation, *The English Catholic Refugees on the Continent, 1559–1795* (New York, 1914), required exhaustive study and research in the archives of Rome, France, and Belgium; in those of Simancas, Seville and Madrid in Spain; and in the libraries and the Public Record Office in England. Thus, not only did he receive a thorough European training but likewise became well acquainted with all the important archives in Europe. Later he was to show how valuable these archives were as sources of American Catholic history. When he returned to America in 1914, he was appointed instructor in history at the Catholic University of America, where he has taught ever since. Fortunately, at the time of his appointment, conditions were more favorable for the establishment of the best methods in the historical disciplines. When the University was opened in 1889, it had a faculty of four foreign scholars, two Germans, one Belgian and one Frenchman. These men brought with them the best in the European tradition and modeled the University along these lines. This tradition was later fostered by the addition to the faculty of two outstanding Catholic scholars who had been educated abroad: Edward Pace who had received his training in the Sorbonne and at Leipzig; and Thomas Shahan who had been trained at Berlin. The beginnings of a department of historical sciences at the University had been made by Shahan before his appointment to the rectorship in 1909. It was under Shahan that Guilday began to revive and enrich the best traditions begun by John Gilmary Shea.

Almost immediately after his appointment, Guilday introduced the seminar; he also was instrumental in founding the

*Catholic Historical Review*, the first issue of which appeared in April, 1915. For the first six years the journal was devoted exclusively to American Church history.[30]  In 1919, Guilday founded the American Catholic Historical Association which has made many important contributions to American Catholic historiography for the past quarter of a century.[31]

Guilday's distinguished contributions to American Church history in the past thirty years have been and are both direct and indirect, and have earned for him the title, Dean of American Catholic Historians.  His two major publications in the field of Catholic Church history have been his *Life and Times of John Carroll, 1735–1815* (2 vols., New York, 1922) ; and his *Life and Times of John England, 1786–1842* (2 vols., New York, 1927). These four volumes represent American Catholic historical scholarship at its best.  Guilday had, from the beginning, recognized and emphasized the importance of the biographical approach to the study of American Church history.[32]  The reason he gave for this was " to center around the great figures in our Church the story of their times with the hope that, as the years pass, our documentary knowledge will be increased and the institutional factors of our Catholic life will become more salient and tangible." [33]  It is not surprising, then, that two of his earlier and major contributions to American Catholic historiography should have been in the difficult field of biography.  Both of these studies are objective treatments of two of the most important figures in the American hierarchy.  Few subjects could have been more difficult for the historian than either Carroll or England, yet Guilday effected in both cases a synthesis of solid fact and a live manner of presentation that will be the model for all historians in the field of Catholic biography.  Based almost entirely on doc-

---

[30] See pp. 57–59.

[31] James J. Kortendick, " Monsignor Peter K. Guilday, Historian of the American Catholic Church," *Catholic Library World*, XII (1940), 263–269.

[32] *Cf.* Peter Guilday, " Guide to the Biographical Sources of the American Hierarchy," *Catholic Historical Review*, V (April, 1919), 120–122.

[33] Kortendick, *loc. cit.*, 267.

umentary materials obtained from the European archives as well as from all the important archives in this country, these volumes have served for years as source-books for the history of the Church in the eastern portion of the United States. Their value in this regard is enhanced considerably by the excellent critical essays on the sources contained in both texts.

With the publication of his *History of the Councils of Baltimore, 1791–1884* (New York, 1932), Guilday furnished Catholic scholars with a one-volume history of the Church for that period. The three Plenary Councils, together with the other nine legislative assemblies convened by Church authority, were national in their influence and reflected the life of the Church throughout the country. Those who participated in them had to deal with existing conditions and urgent problems, and the decrees of the Councils together with the pastoral letters which followed them, form a record of the inner life and growth of Catholicism in the United States. In the pages of his study on the Councils, Guilday, by careful handling of the sources, presents an authoritative and highly readable account of this phase of Catholic history.

As a result of his researches into the life of Carroll, Guilday recognized the high value pastoral letters of the American hierarchy had in reflecting the cultural and social development of the Church. In 1923, he edited *The National Pastorals of the American Hierarchy, 1792–1919* (Washington, D. C., 1923). In 1924 and 1926, he added two more important studies to the literature of American Church history: *The Catholic Church in Virginia 1815–1822* (New York, 1924); [34] and " The Life of John Gilmary Shea." [35] Besides these lengthy studies and his teaching duties at the University, Guilday found time to contribute a large number of scholarly articles to several Catholic publications. Much of the first six volumes of the *Catholic Historical Review* comes from his pen; for example, in Volume VI, besides the documents he edited and the book reviews and notes he wrote, he contributed three valuable essays: " The

---

[34] United States Catholic Historical Society, *Monograph Series,* VIII.
[35] *Historical Records and Studies,* XVII (1926), 1–171.

American Catholic Historical Association;"[36] "The Appointment of Father John Carroll as Prefect-Apostolic of the Church in the New Republic (1783–1785);"[37] and "The Church in the United States (1870–1920). A Retrospect of Fifty Years."[38] Besides his valuable articles on American historiography cited in the preface of this work, some other important magazine studies made by him include: "John Cardinal Farley (1842–1918);"[39] "Father John McKenna: A Loyalist Catholic Priest;"[40] "The Restoration of the Society of Jesus in the United States, 1806–1815;"[41] "Gaetano Bedini: An Episode in the Life of Archbishop John Hughes;"[42] "The Catholic Church in the United States (1776–1926);"[43] "Four Early Ecclesiastical Observers in America;"[44] "The Priesthood of Colonial Maryland (1634–1773);"[45] "Church Reconstruction Under Bishop England, 1822–1842."[46]

The focal point of most of the work Guilday has done during the past thirty years at the University has been his seminar. Here he has developed historical thought after the pattern of the European schools, and has made his department a center for the training of scientific writers in American Church history. His seminar has been a center where the graduate students who worked on individual problems in their fields brought their results for discussion and criticism. The seminar was divided into two periods of one hour each. The first period, Guilday sometimes devoted to some special problem upon which he himself might be engaged at the time such as the revision of one of his own publications; at other times, he would occupy the first

---

36 *Catholic Historical Review*, VI (April, 1920), 3–14.

37 *Ibid.*, (July, 1920), 204–248.

38 *Ibid.*, (Jan., 1921), 533–547.

39 *Catholic World*, CVIII (Nov., 1918), 183–193.

40 *Ibid., CXXXIII* (April, 1931), 21–27.

41 *Records*, XXXII (1921), 177–232.

42 *Historical Records and Studies*, XXIII (1933), 87–170.

43 *Thought*, I (June, 1926), 3–30.

44 *Ecclesiastical Review*, LXXXV (Sept., 1931), 236–254.

45 *Ibid.*, XC (Jan., 1934), 14–31.

46 *Ibid.*, LXVIII (Feb., 1923), 135–147.

hour with lectures on methodology and sources. His volume: *An Introduction to Church History* (St. Louis, 1925) is obviously an outgrowth of his seminar lectures. The second hour was invariably prefaced with a critical review of the historical literature that had come into the offices of the *Catholic Historical Review* during that week. In this manner, the student not only was kept *au courant* of the work being done in other fields, but gained much from Guilday's appraisals. The remainder of the hour, or longer if necessary, was given over to a discussion of the work done by the students with emphasis placed on method and problems of procedure. The student's finished product usually served as his doctoral dissertation or master's thesis. Under these working conditions, Guilday began in 1922 the series *Studies in American Church History.* This series has now reached its thirty-third volume, and, as a whole, represents a large section of the most important research done in the field during the last quarter of a century. Most of the monographs in the series are the first comprehensive, documented accounts of their subjects. Many of the writers have had to construct their studies almost exclusively from archival and manuscript sources, because of the almost total absence of published accounts. The dissertations, in many instances, represent extensive research in local and foreign archives, and hence they have a greater significance because of the light they shed on the archival sources for various phases of Church history in the United States.[47]

---

[47] The thirty-three doctoral dissertations in the series *Studies in American Church History* include: Patrick William Browne, *État de l'Eglise Catholique par Jean Dilhet* (Washington, D. C., 1922); George Boniface Stratemeier, O.P., *Thomas Cornwaleys* (Washington, D. C., 1922); Edward John Hickey, *The Society for the Propagation of the Faith, 1822–1922* (Washington, D. C., 1922); John Hugh O'Donnell, C.S.C., *Catholic Hierarchy in the United States, 1790–1922* (Washington, D. C., 1922); Thomas Patrick O'Rourke, *The Franciscan Missions in Texas, 1690–1793* (Washington, D. C., 1927); Francis Borgia Steck, O.F.M., *Jolliet-Marquette Expedition, 1673* (Washington, D. C., 1927); Claude L. Vogel, O.F.M. Cap., *Capuchins in French Louisiana, 1722–1766* (Washington, D. C., 1928); Sister M. Celeste Leger, *The Catholic Indian Missions in Maine, 1611–1820* (Washington, D. C., 1929); John Kennedy, O.M.I., *Thomas Dongan, 1682–1688* (Washington, D. C., 1930); Sister Helen Louis Nugent, S.N.D.,

Less elaborate are the masters theses that have been the products of this seminar. However, they have an importance all their own since in many instances they are on subjects too narrow in scope to serve as doctoral dissertations and in most cases they

---

*Sister Louis, 1813–1886* (Washington, D. C., 1931); Hugh J. Somers, *Life and Times of Bishop MacDonnel, 1762–1840* (Washington, D. C., 1931); William McNamara, C.S.C., *Catholic Church on the Northern Indiana Frontier, 1791–1844* (Washington, D. C., 1931); Joseph A. Griffin, *Contribution of Belgium to the Catholic Church in America, 1523–1857* (Washington, D. C., 1932); Patrick J. Dignan, *The Legal Incorporation of Church Property in the United States* (Washington, D. C., 1933); Donald C. Shearer, O.F.M.Cap., *Pontificia Americana: A Documentary History of The Catholic Church on the Kentucky Frontier, 1785–1812* (Washington, 1933); Theodore Roemer, O.F.M.Cap., *The Ludwig-Missions-Verein and the Church in the United States, 1838–1918* (Washington, D. C., 1933); Gerald J. Geary, *The Secularization of the California Missions, 1810–1846* (Washington, D. C., 1934); Francis Shaw Guy, *Edmund Bailey O'Callaghan, a Study in American Historiography, 1797–1880* (Washington, D. C., 1934); Fintan G. Walker, *The Catholic Church in the Meeting of Two Frontiers: The Southern Illinois Country, 1763–1793* (Washington, D. C., 1935); Sister M. Regina Baska, O.S.B., *The Benedictine Congregation of St. Scholastica: Its Foundation and Development, 1852–1930* (Washington, D. C., 1935); Jean Delanglez, S.J., *The French Jesuits in Lower Louisiana, 1700–1763* (Washington, D. C., 1935); Joseph W. Ruane, S.S., *The Beginnings of the Society of St. Sulpice in the United States, 1791–1829* (Washington, D. C., 1935); Sister M. Doris Mulvey, O.P., *French Catholic Missionaries in the Present United States, 1604–1791* (Washington, D. C., 1936); Arthur J. Riley, *Catholicism in New England to 1788* (Washington, D. C., 1936); Sister M. Ramona Mattingly, S.C.N., *The Caholic Church on the Kentucky Frontier, 1785–1812* (Washington, D. C., 1936); Sister M. Aquinata Martin, O.P., *The Catholic Church on the Nebraska Frontier, 1854–1885* (Washington, D. C., 1937); Antonio C. Mendoza, A.M., *Historia de la Educacion en Puerto Rico, 1512–1826* (Washington, D. C., 1937); Robert Gorman, *Catholic Apologetical Literature in the United States, 1784–1858* (Washington, D. C., 1939); Vincent F. Holden, C.S.P., *The Early Years of Isaac Thomas Hecker, 1819–1844* (Washington, D. C., 1939); Michael J. Curley, *Church and State in the Spanish Floridas, 1783–1822* (Washington, D. C., 1940); Sister Letitia Mary Lyons, S.H.N., *Francis Norbert Blanchet and the Founding of the Oregon Missions, 1838–1848* (Washington, D. C., 1940); Leo F. Ruskowski, S. S., *French Emigre Priests in the United States, 1791–1815* (Washington, D. C., 1940); Frederick Easterly, C.M., *The Life of Rev. Joseph Rosati, C.M., First Bishop of St. Louis, 1789–1843* (Washington, D. C., 1942).

represent the first fruits of research. Over one hundred of these essays have been directed by Dr. Guilday.[48] The University does not require the printing of the masters theses, but many of them have been published in Catholic historical periodicals giving evidence of their high value as original pieces of research. Some few have been recast and published in book form.

It is difficult to estimate Monsignor Guilday's influence on American Catholic historiography. He is still making contributions to the field and only in recent years have his students been able to show the fruits of their training. He has gained a control of the field of American Church history second to none. During his years of service, he has watched the entire development of American historiography and the part he has played in it by personal correspondence, by personal contact with students of American Church history, as well as by historical productions has been widespread.

Research in American Catholic Church history has not been confined to this one seminar. In the Schools of Theology and Canon Law, and in the Departments of History, Politics, Sociology, Education, and Philosophy, studies have been made in the field of Catholic history under the direction of Monsignori Henry, McCormick, Bernardini, and Jordan, of Professors McCarthy, Purcell, Schaaf, Motry, Stock, Browne, and others.

Since 1920 Richard J. Purcell has been closely associated with Monsignor Guilday in training the students of American Church history in the refined critical methods. A graduate of Yale University in 1916, his dissertation, *Connecticut in Transition* (Washington, D. C., 1918), was awarded the Justin Winsor Prize by the American Historical Association in 1918. From 1931 to 1941, Purcell served as Head of the Department of History at The Catholic University of America. Having done extensive and exhaustive research in Irish antecedents to American history as a Guggenheim Fellow, much of what he has written during the past twenty years has been centered around Irish figures prominent in the United States and immigration. He has contributed about

---

[48] A complete card catalogue of all masters theses is available at the University library.

one hundred annotated articles in secular and Catholic publications and is the author of a text-book in American history entitled: *The American Nation* (Boston, 1929) with later editions.

Purcell's greatest contribution to American Catholic historiography lies in the less easily evaluated efforts he has made through his teaching and direction of research, and innumerable reviews. From his seminar have appeared many important and highly valuable studies bearing on various phases of the history of the Church in the United States. In recent years these researches have been carried into the religious background of American history, particularly into the historical development of Nativism and American Know-nothingism.[49]

In addition the following doctoral students of Professor Purcell have published these important studies which contribute directly or indirectly to the knowledge of American Catholic Church history: Sister Mary Edmund Croghan, R.S.M., *Sisters of Mercy of Nebraska, 1864–1910* (Washington, D. C., 1942) ; Sister M. Frederick Lochemes, *Robert Walsh: His Story* (Washington, D. C., 1941) ; Joseph Francis Thorning, *Religious Liberty in Transition* (Washington, D. C., 1931) ; Sister Mary Angela Fitz-

---

[49] Some of Purcell's series on American Nativism and Know-nothingism follow: a) Doctoral dissertations: Sister M. DeLourdes Gohmann, *Political Nativism in Tennessee* (Washington, D. C., 1938) ; Sister St. Patrick McConville, *Political Nativism in the State of Maryland* (Washington, D. C., 1928) ; Sister Paul of the Cross McGrath, *Political Nativism in Texas* (Washington, D. C., 1930) ; Carroll J. Noonan, Nativism in Connecticut (Washington, D. C., 1938) ; Sister Evangeline Thomas, *Nativism in the Old North-west, 1850–1860* (Washington, D. C., 1936) ; Sister Leonore Fell, *The Foundations of Nativism in American Textbooks, 1783–1860* (Washington, D. C., 1941) ; b) Masters' theses: Sister M. Fabian Buonocore, "Political Nativism in Syracuse, New York;" Mother M. Boniface Henze, "Political Nativism in New Jersey;" Alfred G. Stritch, "Nativism in Cincinnati, 1830–1860;" Sister Agnes Geraldine McGann, "The Know-Nothing Movement in Kentucky in the Fifties;" John Francis Poole, O.P., "The Know-Nothing Movement in Brooklyn;" Sister M. Symphorose Wiodkowska, "Political Nativism in Cleveland, Ohio, to the Civil War;" Sister M. Felicity O'Driscoll, "Political Nativism in Buffalo: 1830–1860;" John Paul Barry, "Know-Nothing Party in the District of Columbia;" Sister M. Xavier Dehner, "The Know-Nothing Party in Virginia, 1852–1860."

morris, *Four Decades of Catholicism in Texas, 1820–1860* (Washington, D. C., 1926); Robert Joseph Dwyer, *The Gentile Comes to Utah, a Study in Religious and Social Conflict, 1862–1890* (Washington, D. C., 1941); Sister M. Aquinas Norton, *Catholic Missionary Activities in the Northwest, 1818–1864* (Washington, D. C., 1930); Sister M. Margaret Jean Kelly, *The Career of Joseph Lane, Frontier Politician* (Washington, D. C., 1942); J. Ryan Beiser, *The Vatican Council and the American Secular Newspapers, 1869–70* (Washington, D. C., 1941); Sister M. Sevina Pahorezki, O.S.F., *The Social and Political Activities of William Joseph Onahan* (Washington, D. C., 1942); Sister M. Theophane Geary, *A History of Third Parties in Pennsylvania, 1840–1860* (Washington, D. C., 1938); Brother Joseph Brennan, *Social Conditions in Industrial Rhode Island: 1820–1860* (Washington, D. C., 1940); Daniel J. Ryan, *American Catholic World War I Records* (Washington, D. C., 1941); Brother J. Robert Lane, F.S.C., *A Political History of Connecticut During the Civil War* (Washington, D. C., 1941); Sister Blanche Marie McEniry, *American Catholics in the War with Mexico* (Washington, D. C., 1937); Sister St. Thomas Aquinas Keefe, *The Congregation of the Grey Nuns: 1737–1910* (Washington, D. C., 1942); Sister M. Claudia Duratschek, *The Beginnings of Catholicism in South Dakota* (Washington, D. C., 1943); Sister M. Virginia Geiger, *Daniel Carroll* (Washington, D. C., 1943); Sister M. Carolyn Klimkenhamer, *Chief Justice White* (Washington, D. C., 1943); J. Walter Coleman, *Labor Disturbances in Pennsylvania, 1850–1880* (Washington, D. C., 1936); Sister M. Stanislaus Connaughton, *The Catholic Telegraph of Cincinnati* (Washington, D. C., 1943); and Peter Beckman, O.S.B., *The Catholic Church in Kansas* (Washington, D. C., 1944).

Over one hundred twenty-five masters' essays, many of which deal with the Catholic element in the American population, have been written under his direction. Purcell himself has not written extensively on any phase of the Church's history. His most important contributions along this line consist of one hundred and seventy-five biographical sketches in the *Dictionary of American Biography*. The majority of these are of personages who have played prominent rôles in the history of American Catholicism; many of them have been superbly done.

Through the graduates of The Catholic University of America the historical seminar system was gradually introduced into other leading Catholic colleges and universities. At none of these schools, however, has there been so intensive a concentration in the field of American Catholic history as at The Catholic University of America. Between the years 1927 and 1941, St. Louis University contributed thirteen doctoral dissertations and fifty masters theses. The work at St. Louis has been of an exceptionally high calibre, largely through the influence of Gilbert J. Garraghan, S.J. and Raymond Corrigan, S.J. Ranking next to St. Louis in the quality of the original research achieved in its historical seminar, is perhaps Creighton University in Omaha. All the work done here in American Church history has been in master's theses. These number only about fourteen, but they are well done, and are worthwhile studies for the Catholic historical scholar to consult. DePaul University and Loyola University of Chicago have each contributed fourteen masters' essays of somewhat less value. Boston College and the University of Notre Dame seem to have introduced the historical seminar at about the same time (1926). The former has contributed to the field of Catholic American history five doctoral studies and some thirty-seven masters', some of them of value. Although Notre Dame has made some forty-nine studies in the field, all masters' essays, the historical seminar there has, more or less, concentrated in secular American history centering around the Middle West.

In the second decade of the twentieth century there appeared two of the earliest and most satisfactory books written in the field of archdiocesan history. The first was John H. Lamott's, *History of the Archdiocese of Cincinnati, 1821–1921* (New York, 1921). A graduate of the Louvain Seminar in History, Lamott handled a most difficult task carefully and well, showing to advantage the critical scholarship and fair-mindedness of the trained historian. His volume, moreover, marked a definite development in method. Up to his time the little diocesan history that was written had been done after the manner of a chronicle. Lamott, however, regarded the archdiocese as a unit instead of a mere aggregate of local parishes. In this orderly and all-embracing program, he followed a chronological, geographical, and institutional development in treating the diversified events of the vast archdiocese.[50]

The second work in this field was done by John E. Rothensteiner (1860–1936). Like Lamott, he too pursued a method of treatment far in advance of all similar works written up to that time. Rothensteiner's early education was obtained in Saint Louis, the city of his birth. His classical, philosophical and theological studies were made at St. Francis Seminary, Milwaukee. Ordained in 1884, he served for a few years in various parishes of the archdiocese, and in 1887 was appointed pastor of St. Michael's Church, Fredericktown, which he held for twenty years. In 1907, he was appointed to the pastorate of Holy Ghost Church, St. Louis, where he remained until his death. In 1934 he was made a domestic prelate. A life-long scholar, Rothensteiner had at the time of his death a splendid library of 16,000 volumes.[51]

Rothensteiner's intensive labors in the field of American Church history began with the establishment in 1915, by the Catholic Union of Missouri, of an Historical Commission for the study of the German Catholics of Missouri. Rothensteiner served on this Commission whose objective was later enlarged to include the general Catholic history of Missouri, irrespective of national origins. When this project failed to make progress, Archbishop Glennon of St. Louis founded the St. Louis Catholic Historical Society. As a member of this society, one of Rothensteiner's earliest projects was the classification of the extensive diocesan collection of documentary material dating from the administration of Bishop Rosati.[52] On this project he was

---

[50] Lamott, *op. cit.*, xiii–xiv.

[51] Thomas F. O'Connor, "John E. Rothensteiner," *Catholic Historical Review*, XXII (Jan., 1937), 432–434. Cf. Sister Mary Callista Campion, "The Life and Works of John Rothensteiner" (Doctoral thesis, University of Illinois, 1940).

[52] The story of the vicissitudes of these archives is interesting. They

ably assisted by the distinguished Catholic historical scholar, Monsignor Frederick G. Holweck.[53] The discovery of this rich collection made the history of the archdiocese of St. Louis possible. Four outstanding scholars rose to the task: Rothensteiner, Holweck, Gilbert J. Garraghan, S.J., and Charles L. Souvay, C.M.[54] By June, 1925, the preliminary study had been sufficiently

had been carefully preserved and added to by Monsignor Henry Van der Sanden, former chancellor of the archdiocese. Van der Sanden had intended them to comprise the source from which he would eventually compile the history of the archdiocese which had long been contemplated. His heavy duties left him no opportunity, and when he retired from the chancery and went to reside at one of the local hospitals, the archives went with him. At his death the archives went to the basement of the hospital where they were most fortunately preserved until located by Rothensteiner and Holweck. *Cf.* O'Connor, *loc. cit.,* 433; F. G. Holweck, "The Historical Archives of the Archdiocese of St. Louis," *St. Louis Catholic History Review,* I (1918), 24–29.

[53] Holweck was a member of the St. Louis Catholic Historical Society and writer in the field of American Church history. His contributions to several Catholic periodicals were largely original pieces of research. His more important studies include: in the *Catholic Historical Review:* "An American Martyrology," VI (Jan., 1921), 495–516; "The Beginnings of the Church in Little Rock," VI (July, 1920), 156–171; "Two Pioneer Indian Priests" (Joseph Kundeck and Joseph Ferneding), *Mid-America,* XII (July, 1929), 63–81; "Reverend Gaspar Henry Ostlangenberg," *Illinois Catholic Historical Review,* III (July, 1920), 43–60; in the *St. Louis Catholic Historical Review:* "The Arkansas Mission under Rosati," I (1919), 243–267; "Rev. John Francis Regis Loisel," I (1919), 103–109; "The Language Question in the Old Cathedral of St. Louis," II (1920), 5–17; "Father Edmond Saulnier," IV (1922), 189–205; "Abbe Joseph Anthony Lutz," V (1923), 183–204; "Public Places of Worship in Saint Louis before Palm Sunday, 1843," IV (1922), 5–12; "Contribution to the Inglesi Affair," V (1923), 14–39.

[54] For Garraghan see pp. 113–116. Souvay (1879–1940) served as editor of the *St. Louis Catholic Historical Review* to which he contributed many excellent articles that have established his reputation in American Catholic historiography. In collaboration with Holweck, he compiled from original sources a *Memorial Sketch of Bishop William Louis Du-Bourg and What His Coming Meant to St. Louis* (St. Louis, 1918); the brochure was edited by Rothensteiner. His valuable contributions to periodicals are: "The Lazarists in Illinois," *Illinois Catholic Historical Review,* I (Jan., 1919), 303–319; in the *Catholic Historical Review,* "Rosati's Election to the Coadjutorship of New Orleans," III (April,

advanced and Rothensteiner was selected to write the history. The field he had to cover was immense and uncharted, and it took him three years to complete the work. " From June 6, 1925," he wrote later, " when I received the commission to write the history of the Archdiocese of St. Louis, until June 5, 1928, when the two massive volumes of the work were nearing completion, I labored most strenuously, by day and far into the night, gathering, sifting, coordinating, and writing down, with the one supreme purpose of giving a true, clear and exhaustive account of the work of God done by men and women, bishops, priests and laymen, in the vast territory of the Mississippi valley." [55]

The two volume *History of the Archdiocese of St. Louis* (St. Louis, 1928) gave evidence of exhaustive research and, like the work of Lamott, was an important contribution to the methodology of diocesan history. The method Rothensteiner followed in synthesizing a tremendously large subject was to divide it into three parts: Part I deals with the beginnings and embraces the events from Marquette's voyage to the erection of the diocese of St. Louis under Bishop Rosati, 1673–1827; Part II treats the diocese of St. Louis, embracing the events from the division of the diocese of Louisiana into the dioceses of St. Louis and New Orleans, until the erection of St. Louis into an archdiocese under Peter Richard Kenrick, 1827–1847; Part III is concerned with the archdiocese of St. Louis and covers the period from 1847–1927.

The selection of Rothensteiner was largely due to the ability he had shown in the field as early as 1917. His *The Chronicles*

---

1917), 3–21; (July, 1917), 165–186; "A Centennial of the Church in St. Louis (1818–1918)," IV (April, 1918), 52–75; " Questions Anent Mother Seton's Conversion," V (July–Oct., 1919), 223–238; " The Society of St. Vincent de Paul as an Agency of Reconstruction," VII (Jan., 1922), 441–457; in the *St. Louis Catholic Historical Review:* "Rummaging through Old Parish Records; an Historical Sketch of the Church of Lafayette, La., 1821–1921," III (1921), 242–294; " Episcopal Visitation of the Diocese of New Orleans, 1827–1828," I (1919), 215–230; " DuBourg and the Biblical Society," II (1920), 18–25; " Around the St. Louis Cathedral with Bishop DuBourg, 1818–1820," V (1923), 149–159. In 1933, Souvay was made Superior General of the Congregation of the Mission with residence in Paris.

[55] O'Connor, *loc. cit.,* 434.

of an Old Mission Parish (St. Louis, 1917); *P. Bernard Von Limpach und die Anfänge der Kirche in St. Louis* (St. Louis, 1918), and *Der erste deutsch-amerikanishe Priester des Westens, Geschichtliche Stunde* (St. Louis, 1918)—a study of Paul de Saint Pierre, were all well-written monographs. In the prosecution of his preliminary studies he contributed a number of scholarly articles to several historical quarterlies. These studies, like the articles of Holweck, Souvay and Garraghan, were of a more detailed and exhaustive nature than the limits of space permitted him to incorporate later into his history. Exclusive of his biographical sketches the articles of permanent importance to the student of Catholic origins in the West include: " Archbishop Eccleston of Baltimore and the Visitandines' Foundation at Kaskaskia; " [56] " The Northeastern Part of the Diocese of St. Louis under Bishop Rosati; " [57] " Historical Antecedents of the Diocese of St. Louis; " [58] " The Sulpicians in the Illinois Country; " [59] " From Chicago to St. Louis in the Early Dawn of Western History; " [60] " Historical Sketch of Catholic New Madrid; " [61] " Early Missionary Efforts Among the Indians in the Diocese of St. Louis." [62]

No aspect of historical study in the United States has given proof of more serious work than the study of American Catholic history during the past generation. In this period a singularly large amount of work has appeared, showing a marked advance in Catholic historical scholarship. Most of the writers of this era have confined their researches to certain localities in preparation for larger, more definitive studies. The most notable of these regional writers are: Thomas F. Meehan for New York, Joseph J. Thompson for Iillinois, Matthias M. Hoffmann for Iowa, Francis E. Tourscher and John M. Lenhart for Pennsylvania, Frederick

---

[56] *Illinois Catholic Historical Review,* I (1918), 500–509.

[57] *Ibid.,* II (1919), 175–195, 269–285, 396–416; III (1921), 61–72, 126–145, 285–302, 389–403; IV (1922), 34–42, 135–153.

[58] *Ibid.,* IV (1922), 243–254.

[59] *Ibid.,* VIII (1926), 244–249.

[60] *Ibid.,* IX (1927), 21–38.

[61] *St. Louis Catholic Historical Review,* IV (1922), 113–129, 206–218.

[62] *Ibid.,* II (1920), 57–96.

J. Zwierlein for Rochester, New York, Jean Delanglez, Francis Borgia Steck, Thomas McAvoy, Peter Leo Johnson and Felix Fellner, for the Middle West, Edwin V. O'Hara for the Far West, Paul J. Foik for the Southwest, and Michael Kenny for the Southeast.

Although belonging in a sense to this group of regional writers, Gilbert J. Garraghan, S.J., (1871–1942) did so much for American Catholic historical scholarship that he deserves a more extensive treatment. Born in Chicago, he joined the Society of Jesus in 1890. Attending the historic St. Stanislaus Seminary, Florissant, Missouri, he lived and studied in the tradition of the founders and pioneer members of the Missouri Province of the Society of Jesus. It was here that he became familiar with the names of those whom he was later to make his life study—Van Quickenborne, Van Assche DeSmet and Van de Velde. From 1901 to 1905, Garraghan pursued his theological studies at St. Louis School of Divinity and was ordained to the priesthood in 1904. In 1906–1907, he taught at Creighton University and from 1907 to 1911 at St. Stanislaus Seminary, Florissant. Returning to St. Louis, he held the office of socius to the Provincial from 1911 to 1921. While living at St. Louis University he had at his command the rich archival collections of that institution and his position as socius gave him access to the archives of the other institutions of the Society located within the jurisdiction of the Province. Moreover, the chief mid-western depositories of documents, secular and religious, were all within relatively easy reach. And it was at about this time that the precious St. Louis archdiocesan archives were rescued and their treasure made available to scholars.

About the beginning of the second decade of the present century, Garraghan began to publish a succession of monographs and books dealing with the history of the Church in the Middle West. The earliest of these volumes was *Catholic Beginnings in Kansas City, Missouri: an Historical Sketch* (Chicago, 1920). Written primarily from the letters and reports of the pioneer missionaries to their superiors, it is still a necessary work for those who would adequately understand the complex elements entering into the development of the Missouri-Kansas frontier. In this initial volume he displayed two characteristics of all his later works, namely, a persevering effort to base his narrative as far as possible on primary sources, and to integrate the story of Catholic activity with the general history of the time and place.[63] This study was followed a year later by *The Catholic Church in Chicago, 1673–1871, an Historical Sketch* (Chicago, 1921). Garraghan resorted to original sources for this work also, but since the fire of 1871 had damaged a large amount of the ecclesiastical records of Chicago, he had to rely to some extent on secondary accounts for the later chapters. This volume also indicated the significant advance that had been made in the writing of diocesan histories. The first four chapters are excellent examples for future writers in this field to follow in sifting and interweaving all relevant archival material into the narrative of their works.

In 1923, Garraghan made another significant contribution to American Catholic historiography with one of the best-constructed parish histories that has been written. The volume was entitled *Saint Ferdinand de Florissant, the Story of an Ancient Parish* (Chicago, 1923) and was an account of the simple beginnings of far-reaching religious enterprises.

The decade following the publication of this work, Garraghan devoted to research in the history of the Church and of his Society in the Middle West. No volume came from his pen during these years, but he contributed a large number of preliminary studies to various historical journals. Some of these studies are definitive treatments of important aspects of Western Catholic history, notably: " The Trappists of Monks Mound; "[64] " The Ecclesiastical Rule of Old Quebec in Mid-America; "[65] " John Anthony Grassi, 1775–1849; "[66] " Earliest Settlements of the Illinois Country; "[67] " Samuel Charles Mazzuchelli, Dominican of the

---

[63] Thomas F. O'Connor, " Gilbert J. Garraghan, S.J., Historian," *Historical Bulletin*, XXI (1943), 54.

[64] *Records*, XXXVI (1925), 70–110.

[65] *Catholic Historical Review*, XIX (April, 1933), 17–32.

[66] *Ibid.*, XXIII (Oct., 1937), 273–292.

[67] *Ibid.*, XV (Jan., 1930), 351–362.

Frontier;"[68] " Catholic Beginnings in Chicago;"[69] " Old Vincennes; a Chapter in the Ecclesiastical History of the West;"[70] " A Jesuit Westward Movement;"[71] " New Lights on Old Cahokia;"[72] " The Emergence of the Missouri Valley into History."[73]

In 1934, he republished a select number of these researches in *Chapters on Frontier History: Research Studies in the Making of the West* (Milwaukee, 1934). As an active member of the St. Louis Catholic Historical Society, Garraghan, having access to the Jesuit records at St. Louis University, did much of the preliminary work for Rothensteiner's history of the archdiocese. Likewise, his years as editor of *Mid-America* (1929–1934) were notable in the history of that scholarly quarterly. In the midst of these activities, Garraghan kept gathering the materials for his monumental work, *The Jesuits in the Middle United States* (3 vols., New York, 1938). The absence of printed accounts bearing in any significant way on the history of the mid-western Jesuits made it necessary for Garraghan to derive his material almost entirely from original and unpublished sources. For this work he used as sources the general archives of the Society of Jesus, the archives of the Jesuit provinces of Missouri, Maryland-New York, Northern Belgium, and Lower Germany, the Baltimore and St. Louis archdiocesan archives, the archives of the University of Notre Dame, and the files of the Indian Office, Department of the Interior, Washington, as well as numerous other archival depositories.[74]

A significant and permanent contribution to American Catholic historiography has come from the pen of one of the more talented of the younger historians in the country. Carlos E. Castañeda (1896–    ) was born in Mexico and was educated at the University of Texas, William and Mary College, and the

---

[68] *Mid-America*, XX (1938), 253–262.
[69] *Ibid.*, XVI (July, 1933), 33–44.
[70] *Ibid.*, XIII (April, 1931), 324–340.
[71] *Ibid.*, XVIII (1936), 165–181.
[72] *Illinois Catholic Historical Review*, XI (Oct., 1928), 99–146.
[73] *Ibid.*, IX (April, 1927), 306–322.
[74] O'Connor, " Garraghan," 53–54.

University of Mexico. A librarian, bibliographer and historian, he was appointed historiographer of the Knights of Columbus Historical Commission shortly after its organization in 1923. His researches into history have been centered around the mission era in the Southwest. As a member of the Historical Commission, Castañeda was only one of a group of eminent scholars who by co-operation and collaboration made possible the largest single project executed in the field of American Catholic historiography. The seven volume work on the history of the Church in Texas, entitled *Our Catholic Heritage in Texas, 1519–1936* (Austin, Texas, 1936–    ), is the most monumental project that has been attempted in the field. For over ten years the Commission gathered documents from all over the world and made preliminary studies for the more intensive research that followed. With the additional aid of many basic studies made by Herbert E. Bolton and others during the past thirty years and the large mass of new documentary sources recently discovered, Castañeda achieved an admirable synthesis of Texas history in all its aspects. In the sifting of the great output of articles, documents, and monographs and incorporating them into a readable narrative, he has achieved the same high standard of historical scholarship as Guilday and Garraghan and like them has marked a milestone in the advance of American Catholic historiography.

The latest important contributions to American Church historiography have been coming from the pen of Theodore Maynard. Among his published works in this field, special attention should be given to his *The Story of American Catholicism* (New York, 1941) wherein he presents the history of the Church in a challenging, provocative, and readable manner. Although Maynard belongs essentially to that class known as " literary " historians or " popularizers," his works are to be taken seriously by the critical historians because of their readableness and the appeal they have to students of Church history everywhere. All the faults common to writers of popular history can be charged to Dr. Maynard. All his works suffer from a lack of proportion, a tone of personal conviction and frequent excursions into realms other than history brought about largely by the selection of material which lends itself best to literary treatment. In spite of these defects, however, his volumes have considerable worth and literary charm. His place in American Catholic historiography would be more secure if he would be more meticulous in sifting his evidence and concealing some of his antipathies.

# INDEX

# THE AMERICAN
# CATHOLIC TRADITION

*An Arno Press Collection*

Callahan, Nelson J., editor. **The Diary of Richard L. Burtsell, Priest of New York.** 1978

Curran, Robert Emmett. **Michael Augustine Corrigan and the Shaping of Conservative Catholicism in America, 1878-1902.** 1978

Ewens, Mary. **The Role of the Nun in Nineteenth-Century America** (Doctoral Thesis, The University of Minnesota, 1971). 1978

McNeal, Patricia F. **The American Catholic Peace Movement 1928-1972** (Doctoral Dissertation, Temple University, 1974). 1978

Meiring, Bernard Julius. **Educational Aspects of the Legislation of the Councils of Baltimore, 1829-1884** (Doctoral Dissertation, University of California, Berkeley, 1963). 1978

Murnion, Philip J., **The Catholic Priest and the Changing Structure of Pastoral Ministry, New York, 1920-1970** (Doctoral Dissertation, Columbia University, 1972). 1978

White, James A., **The Era of Good Intentions: A Survey of American Catholics' Writing Between the Years 1880-1915** (Doctoral Thesis, University of Notre Dame, 1957). 1978

Dyrud, Keith P., Michael Novak and Rudolph J. Vecoli, editors. **The Other Catholics.** 1978

Gleason, Philip, editor. **Documentary Reports on Early American Catholicism.** 1978

Bugg, Lelia Hardin, editor. **The People of Our Parish.** 1900

Cadden, John Paul. **The Historiography of the American Catholic Church: 1785-1943.** 1944

Caruso, Joseph. **The Priest.** 1956

Congress of Colored Catholics of the United States. **Three Catholic Afro-American Congresses.** [1893]

Day, Dorothy. **From Union Square to Rome.** 1940

Deshon, George. **Guide for Catholic Young Women.** 1897

Dorsey, Anna H[anson]. **The Flemmings.** [1869]

Egan, Maurice Francis. **The Disappearance of John Longworthy.** 1890

Ellard, Gerald. **Christian Life and Worship.** 1948

England, John. **The Works of the Right Rev. John England, First Bishop of Charleston.** 1849. 5 vols.

Fichter, Joseph H. **Dynamics of a City Church.** 1951

Furfey, Paul Hanly. **Fire on the Earth.** 1936

Garraghan, Gilbert J. **The Jesuits of the Middle United States.** 1938. 3 vols.

Gibbons, James. **The Faith of Our Fathers.** 1877

Hecker, I[saac] T[homas]. **Questions of the Soul.** 1855

Houtart, François. **Aspects Sociologiques Du Catholicisme Américain.** 1957

[Hughes, William H.] **Souvenir Volume. Three Great Events in the History of the Catholic Church in the United States.** 1889

[Huntington, Jedediah Vincent]. **Alban: A Tale of the New World.** 1851

**Kelley, Francis C., editor. The First American Catholic Missionary Congress.** 1909

Labbé, Dolores Egger. **Jim Crow Comes to Church.** 1971

LaFarge, John. **Interracial Justice.** 1937

Malone, Sylvester L. **Dr. Edward McGlynn.** 1918

**The Mission-Book of the Congregation of the Most Holy Redeemer.** 1862

O'Hara, Edwin V. **The Church and the Country Community.** 1927

Pise, Charles Constantine. **Father Rowland.** 1829

Ryan, Alvan S., editor. **The Brownson Reader.** 1955

Ryan, John A., **Distributive Justice.** 1916

Sadlier, [Mary Anne]. **Confessions of an Apostate.** 1903

**Sermons Preached at the Church of St. Paul the Apostle, New York, During the Year 1863.** 1864

Shea, John Gilmary. **A History of the Catholic Church Within the Limits of the United States.** 1886/1888/1890/1892. 4 Vols.

Shuster, George N. **The Catholic Spirit in America.** 1928

Spalding, J[ohn] L[ancaster]. **The Religious Mission of the Irish People and Catholic Colonization.** 1880

Sullivan, Richard. **Summer After Summer.** 1942

[Sullivan, William L.] **The Priest.** 1911

Thorp, Willard. **Catholic Novelists in Defense of Their Faith, 1829-1865.** 1968

Tincker, Mary Agnes. **San Salvador.** 1892

Weninger, Franz Xaver. **Die Heilige Mission** *and* **Praktische Winke Für Missionare.** 1885. 2 Vols. in 1

Wissel, Joseph. **The Redemptorist on the American Missions.** 1920. 3 Vols. in 2

**The World's Columbian Catholic Congresses and Educational Exhibit.** 1893

Zahm, J[ohn] A[ugustine]. **Evolution and Dogma.** 1896